# LEICESTERSHIRE

Edited by Donna Samworth

First published in Great Britain in 2003 by
*YOUNG WRITERS*
Remus House,
Coltsfoot Drive,
Peterborough, PE2 9JX
Telephone  (01733) 890066

SB ISBN 1 84460 295 8

# FOREWORD

Young Writers was established in 1991 as a foundation for promoting the reading and writing of poetry amongst children and young adults. Today it continues this quest and proceeds to nurture and guide the writing talents of today's youth.

From this year's competition Young Writers is proud to present a showcase of the best poetic talent from across the UK. Each hand-picked poem has been carefully chosen from over 66,000 'Hullabaloo!' entries to be published in this, our eleventh primary school series.

This year in particular we have been wholeheartedly impressed with the quality of entries received. The thought, effort, imagination and hard work put into each poem impressed us all and once again the task of editing was a difficult but enjoyable experience.

We hope you are as pleased as we are with the final selection and that you and your family will continue to be entertained with *Hullabaloo! Leicestershire* for many years to come.

# CONTENTS

### Newbold CE Primary School

| | |
|---|---|
| Aimee Odendaal  (10) | 35 |
| Kendall McEwan  (10) | 36 |
| Joanna Emily Louise Peat  (8) | 36 |
| Sean Peat  (10) | 37 |
| Carys Gidlow  (8) | 37 |
| Michael Mannion  (10) | 38 |
| Nancy Ella Waldrum  (8) | 38 |
| Sian Summerfield  (9) | 39 |
| Thomas Bale  (9) | 39 |
| Harry Miles  (9) | 40 |
| Jessica Fardoe  (10) | 40 |
| Thomas David Renton  (11) | 41 |
| Stefan Beniston  (10) | 41 |
| Rhiannon Winlow  (10) | 42 |

### Newcroft CP School

| | |
|---|---|
| Katie Hutchinson  (10) | 42 |
| Neha Puntambekar  (10) | 43 |
| Ellie Bennett  (8) | 44 |
| Charlotte Woods  (10) | 44 |
| Kerry Exon  (10) | 45 |
| Jade Beedham  (9) | 45 |
| Beth Wright  (10) | 46 |
| Rachael Burton  (9) | 47 |

### Newton Burgoland Primary School

| | |
|---|---|
| Cameron Hirons  (9) | 47 |
| Bethan Jacka  (8) | 48 |
| Sara Green  (8) | 49 |
| Hannah Barnes  (9) | 50 |
| Joshua Carr  (7) | 51 |
| Carl Baillie  (10) | 51 |
| Rameeka Banning  (8) | 52 |
| Drew Fores  (7) | 52 |
| Glynn Ruddock  (11) | 53 |
| Daniel White  (9) | 54 |
| Liam Reeves  (11) | 55 |

| | |
|---|---:|
| Hannah Robinson  (10) | 56 |
| Edward Storer  (11) | 57 |
| Ryan Ruddock  (9) | 58 |
| Tony Watts  (10) | 58 |
| Matthew Jacka  (10) | 59 |
| Laura Green  (10) | 60 |

### Normanton-on-Soar Primary School

| | |
|---|---:|
| Maneet Sagoo  (10) | 60 |
| Jennifer Harrison  (11) | 61 |
| Kyle Carlisle-Sankey  (10) | 61 |
| Matthew Hawes  (9) | 62 |
| James Wilks  (10) | 62 |
| Joe Toon  (10) | 63 |
| Francesca Hibbins  (9) | 63 |
| Cathryn Brain  (10) | 64 |
| Paul Johnson  (10) | 64 |
| Danielle Evans  (11) | 65 |
| Christopher Hellier  (9) | 65 |
| Holly Bishop  (10) | 65 |

### Orchard Community Primary School

| | |
|---|---:|
| Adrian Cox  (9) | 66 |
| Jack Brownett  (10) | 67 |
| Katie Rebecca Lewis  (9) | 68 |
| Harriet Brown  (10) | 68 |
| Dane Barwell  (9) | 69 |
| Oliver James Tarpey  (9) | 70 |
| Matthew Cox  (10) | 70 |
| Sarah-Jane Louise Doherty  (10) | 71 |
| Thomas Goodge  (9) | 72 |
| Edward Foweather  (9) | 73 |
| Steven Kirton  (10) | 74 |
| Matthew Rolley  (9) | 75 |
| Joshua-Thomas Wilkinson  (9) | 76 |
| Jake Barker  (10) | 77 |
| Guy Williams  (9) | 78 |
| Bethany Ann Homer  (9) | 79 |

| | |
|---|---|
| Lyndsay Elks  (10) | 80 |
| Craig Nash  (10) | 81 |
| James Curtis  (10) | 82 |
| Gemma Baldy  (9) | 82 |
| Michael Sheehan  (10) | 83 |
| Sophie Tyler  (9) | 83 |
| Sophie Bucknall  (9) | 84 |
| Ryan Oakley  (9) | 84 |
| Patrick Dawson  (10) | 85 |
| James Elkins  (10) | 85 |
| Helen Sleigh  (10) | 86 |

### St Bartholomew's CE Primary School, Loughborough

| | |
|---|---|
| Lauren Bestwick  (10) | 86 |
| Joshua Selby  (11) | 87 |
| Alex Eaton  (10) | 87 |
| Harry Collinson  (9) | 88 |
| Sophie Middleton  (9) | 89 |
| Damon Barber  (9) | 90 |
| Bryony Unwin  (10) | 91 |
| Laurie Anderson  (9) | 92 |
| Edward Rusak-Plant  (8) | 93 |
| Ben Sinfield  (10) | 93 |
| Daniel Barby  (9) | 94 |
| Laura Connolly  (8) | 95 |
| Isabelle Carter  (9) | 96 |
| Emma Russell  (8) | 96 |
| Holly Lacey  (8) | 97 |
| Felicity Norris  (9) | 98 |
| Christopher Swain  (8) | 99 |
| John Timerick  (8) | 99 |
| Ryan Beecham  (8) | 100 |
| Pedram Amirkhalili  (9) | 100 |
| Tom Parslow  (8) | 101 |
| Timothy Barrass  (8) | 101 |
| John Vale  (9) | 102 |
| Hannah Iley  (10) | 103 |
| Matthew Watson  (10) | 104 |

| | |
|---|---|
| Harry Newcombe  (9) | 104 |
| Lauren Beech  (8) | 105 |
| Charlotte Robinson  (8) | 105 |
| Kate Smith  (8) | 106 |
| Sophie Parslow  (10) | 106 |
| Ursula Rae  (11) | 107 |
| Ryan Hopewell  (10) | 107 |
| Sam Russell  (11) | 108 |
| Emily Richards  (10) | 108 |
| Dan Mousley  (9) | 109 |
| Ben Taylor  (10) | 109 |
| Joel Hardcastle  (9) | 110 |
| Edward Mear  (11) | 110 |
| Joshua Kirk  (10) | 111 |
| Sophie Foster  (8) | 111 |
| Leo May  (11) | 112 |
| Naomi Shipway  (11) | 112 |
| Hannah Brennan-Mee  (11) | 113 |
| Nathalie Dawson  (11) | 113 |
| Harry Thirlby  (9) | 114 |
| Stephen Maddocks  (10) | 114 |
| Rachel McCoubrie  (11) | 115 |
| Caleb Roberts  (10) | 115 |
| Bethany Coy  (11) | 116 |
| Amy Paramore  (9) | 116 |
| Toby Steel  (10) | 117 |
| Jack Graham  (10) | 117 |
| Max Wootton  (10) | 118 |
| Ross Gartshore  (10) | 118 |
| Hannah Wilson  (10) | 119 |
| Alex Francis  (10) | 120 |
| Gemma Adkin  (10) | 121 |
| Alex Honour  (11) | 121 |
| Thomas Hayes  (10) | 122 |
| Gemma Barby  (11) | 122 |
| Calum Rae  (9) | 123 |
| Annabel Moore  (10) | 123 |
| Kerrie Laverick  (10) | 124 |

| Jessica Jenkinson (11) | 149 |
| Lucy Fergusson (9) | 150 |
| Rebecca Peat (9) | 151 |
| Jack Tranter (9) | 152 |
| Abigail Morris (9) | 153 |
| Beth Hushon (10) | 154 |
| Emily Haynes (10) | 155 |
| Wesley Boucher (10) | 156 |

### St Paul's CE Primary School, Woodhouse Eaves

| Anthony Luckham (8) | 156 |
| Amelia Selby (7) | 157 |
| Nusaybah Al-Mansouri (8) | 157 |
| Adam Spooner (8) | 157 |
| Daisy Halligan (8) | 158 |
| Sophie Lindeman (7) | 158 |
| Kim Quilter (8) | 158 |
| Rosalind Barlow (7) | 159 |
| Harriet Lavender (7) | 159 |
| Alice Lathbury (8) | 159 |
| Maxine Hunter (8) | 160 |
| Killian Kirkpatrick (7) | 160 |
| Charlie Keightley (7) | 160 |
| Clarice Elliott (7) | 161 |
| Natasha Hicks (8) | 161 |
| Jack Harding (7) | 161 |
| Natalie Condron (7) | 162 |
| Oliver Hamilton (7) | 162 |
| Matthew Bettany (7) | 162 |
| Adeana Button (7) | 163 |
| Hannah Allsopp (7) | 163 |
| Charlie Breed (8) | 163 |

### Sketchley Hill Primary School

| Chloe Boulton (8) | 164 |
| Jack Varden (8) | 164 |
| Amy Richardson (8) | 165 |
| Liam Burchell (8) | 165 |

| | |
|---|---|
| Luke Pegg (10) | 182 |
| Gemma Jackson (10) | 182 |
| Carrie-Anne Judge (9) | 183 |
| Kharen Amella Birch (10) | 183 |
| Alyssa Hunt (9) | 184 |
| Melissa Woolley (10) | 184 |
| Liam Henson (9) | 185 |
| Nakita McDonnagh (10) | 185 |
| Matthew Quigley (9) | 186 |
| Georgina Parker (10) | 186 |
| Heidi Lee (11) | 187 |
| Stephanie Pownall (11) | 187 |
| Lauren Esders (9) | 188 |
| Zara Bridges (9) | 188 |
| Monica Matharu (8) | 188 |
| Sophie Brinkworth (10) | 189 |
| Jodie Taylor (9) | 189 |
| Micaela Vallance (10) | 189 |
| Charlotte Linford (9) | 190 |
| Matthew Beeby (9) | 191 |
| Kallum Jamieson (10) | 192 |
| Charlotte Simms (10) | 192 |
| Ben Brooks (8) | 193 |
| Jessicalin Harvey (8) | 193 |
| Amy Welstead (10) | 194 |
| Jennifer Smith (10) | 194 |
| Rosie Sutton (10) | 194 |
| Danielle Preston (10) | 195 |
| Ryan Mitchell (10) | 195 |

# The Poems

# A LIFE OF WATER

*Spring*
> Bubbles out of the boggy ground
> Then trickles down the rocky slope
> Like a slithering snake
> Like a hunting leopard.

*Stream*
> Flowing round the jagged rocks
> As it picks up speed
> Like a racing greyhound.

*River*
> As it rapidly flies past
> It dodges and weaves round the huge rocks
> Like a footballer dribbling to goal.

*Sea*
> Humungous waves crash back down
> So bubbles form.
> Waves form, one, two reaching out,
> Leaping to get you.

**Jimmy Madden  (10)**

## THE VOODOO CURSE

As I stepped up to the broken wall,
The ancient stones began to fall.

Never knowing what comes next,
What will happen, what are the affects?

Creepy statues come alive
As I reach the voodoo hive.

My greed decides to reach my bones
As I decide to take the sacred stones.

As I touch the silvery treasure
The curse gives the opposite of pleasure.

*The wall begins to fall.*

**Jared Payne (10)**


## THE MAN FROM CHINA

There was a man from China,
Who thought he was a mountain climber.
He fell on a rock and
Split his head in shock.
Now he's bled and covered with red,
The doctors said, 'He's dead.'
They took him to the ground,
Where they buried him with no sound.
The man who bled is certainly dead,
Because he cracked his head.

**Dean Koash (10)**
**Belvoirdale County Primary School**

## AN OWL OF THE NIGHT

There is an owl
Flying in the moonlight
There is an owl
An owl of the night.

Its wings are so wide
Rats and rabbits
Shake and hide.

It prowls around the forest
Looking for prey
Comes out a night
Asleep by day.

*Lorna Dingwall  (9)*
**Church Langton Primary School**


## WHAT IS A CLOUD?

A cloud is a sheet
Separating Heaven from Earth.

A cloud is a giant angel
Passing the land and sea.

A cloud is a snow waterfall.

A cloud is a flock of doves
High in the sky.

A cloud is feathers
Falling from Heaven.

*Eddie Heritage  (10)*
**Church Langton Primary School**

## MY RABBIT HOLLY

She is the sweet melody of the harp,
A night full of twinkling stars,
The colour of a pale calm blue.
She is a fluffy velvet lilac cushion
A feel of happiness that goes on forever
The taste of fudge and chocolate ice cream.
She is the rare sight of a Rafflesia Arnoldi.
She is mine.

*Sorcha McCole  (9)*
**Church Langton Primary School**


## THE QUEEN

She is the colour silver,
A swift tune played on a harp,
A comfy settee soft and cosy,
She is the soft touch of snow,
She is a gentle ballerina.

*Zoe-Anne Thorpe  (10)*
**Church Langton Primary School**


## MY MUM

She is the colour blue
She is the scene of a garden full of flowers
She is the weather, sunny and calm
She is a squirrel
She is a love book

*Rory Jakeman  (9)*
**Church Langton Primary School**

## HARRIET

She is the mellow colour yellow
A lively dolphin splashing in a sea
       of happiness.
She is a sweet strawberry milkshake
       bubbly and frothy.
A pair of combats and a lilac top.
She is an action book full of adventure.

*Emilia Rose Baker (10)*
**Church Langton Primary School**


## THE QUEEN

The Queen is a gentle breeze in April
All the colours are hers
A scene of happiness, peace and comfort
She is an intelligent animal, just and loyal
(But on the other side of her)
She is a knowledgeable, adventurous book
A royal horse and carriage is she.

*Olivia Jakeman*
**Church Langton Primary School**


## CLOWNS - HAIKU

Acrobatic clowns
Jumping, twisting in the air.
Slowing in action.

*Georgia Skupinski (9)*
**Church Langton Primary School**

## I'D LIKE TO PAINT

I'd like to paint the smell of ripened gooseberries,
The feel of air, the taste of melting chocolate.
I'd like to paint the feel of the ground shaking,
When the rainbow falls from the sky.
I'd like to paint the taste of my favourite food,
The sound of children, the sound of a crocodile slowing moving
Through rippling water, to catch its prey.
I'd like to paint my friend's soul, God's power and
The sound of the salty sea drawing back the sand.

*Tim Spencer (9)*
*Church Langton Primary School*


## THE WRAITH OF THE NIGHT

The white figure,
An arrow shooting through the night
Eyes examining here and there
The wraith, hunter, king of the air
A gust of wind ruffles the rabbits' fur.
The rabbit can see the future
It sees its death.

*Charles Faye (9)*
*Church Langton Primary School*


## WINTER - HAIKU

The world all asleep.
Cold winds mock the early buds.
Freezing them to death.

*Ryan Smith (10)*
*Church Langton Primary School*

## MY FRIEND EMMA

She is the colour fluorescent pink
A bouncing newborn lamb
A pale blue limousine speeding quickly, quickly,
        down the highway.
She is a bud bursting in spring
She's a relaxing harp mixed with an energetic guitar.
She is the scent of chips from the chip shop.

*Harriet Currie (10)*
*Church Langton Primary School*


## SEASONS OF ICE AND SNOW

W inter, season of ice and snow
I   cicles like frozen tears falling off the roof
N  ature sleeps when white snow falls
T   rees covered in a soft quilt of snow
E   erie and cold is the air
R  ain like diamonds falling out of the sky.

*William Webb (9)*
*Church Langton Primary School*


## FIRE - CINQUAIN

Dazzling
Roaring, raging
Spreading, burning, trapping
Destroying, intoxicating
Danger!

*Lauren Harvison (10)*
*Church Langton Primary School*

# THE MIDNIGHT HORSE

When the wind is blowing frantically,
And the sound of thunder's wild,
The midnight horse is the sound you hear.
As she rides through the sky with her tail of lightning,
Whipping up the sky like a Milky Way,
And she pulls up the clouds with her moonlit hooves,
As the sun comes and the shadows disappear,
She goes to rest in the heavens until another stormy night.

*Megan Reddi (10)*
*Church Langton Primary School*

# WHAT IS . . . PLUTO?

God's bowling ball
Circling around the blazing sun.
A circular ice cube
Imprisoned in dark space.
A roaring winter wind
Destroying all existence.

*James Fennemore (10)*
*Church Langton Primary School*

# ANGER

A vast colossal
Giant among giants
Burning into me.

*Angus Clarke (9)*
*Church Langton Primary School*

## A FRIGHT FOR THE NIGHT

Night awakes
Dark and damp
Streaks of light
Come from a cloud of night
Master of air
Master of night
Comes out from his lair
Wind whining and whistling
Through his wings
Death is in the air
His prey singing in terror
Creatures return to hide
Death is in the air.

*Peter Kearvell-White  (8)*
**Church Langton Primary School**


## I'D LIKE TO PAINT

I'd like to paint . . .

The smell of freshly baked bread,
The sound of my friends laughing,
The sound of rain falling from the sky,
The touch of a feather tickling my neck,
The sound of a book opening,
The colours of Heaven,
The wind running through my hair,
The smell of chocolate,
The sound of my dog.

*Alexandra Hardy  (9)*
**Church Langton Primary School**

# CHARGE OF THE CHILD BRIGADE
*(Based on 'The Charge Of The Light Brigade' by Alfred Lord Tennyson)*

Half a step, half a step,
Half a step onward
Into the classroom of death
Step the six hundred.

Forward the child brigade
Charge for the teachers
Capture the answers
Onward they run
Teachers to the right of them
Teachers to the left of them
Oh the wild charge they made
Noble six hundred.

***George H Robinson (10)***
**Church Langton Primary School**


# THE MOON IS . . .

A huge boulder
Tumbling down from God's mine.
A silver sixpence
Glowing as it spins.
A ghostly sail on a black backdrop
An angel floating down from Heaven
Sent to shine upon us.

***Joseph Bladon (10)***
**Church Langton Primary School**

## CHARGE OF RUGBY BRIGADE
*(Based on 'The Charge Of The Light Brigade' by Alfred Lord Tennyson)*

Half a try, half a try,
Half a try onward.
All on the pitch of death,
Trudged the six hundred.
Players to the right of them,
Players to the left of them.
All on the pitch of death,
Charged the six hundred.

'Go score a try for us,
Charge for the line,' he said.
Crowd to the right of them,
Crowd to the left of them.
All on the pitch of death,
Noble six hundred.

***Louis J Marshall  (10)***
**Church Langton Primary School**


## MY GRAN

My gran is as cuddly as a koala
Her hair is like a polar bear's skin
Her eyes are like sapphires sparkling in the sunlight
Her face is like a wrinkled plastic bag
When she walks she is like a penguin as she moves slowly
When she sits she is like a teddy bear
When she laughs she is like a hyena with her everlasting laugh
When she sleeps she is like a hedgehog in hibernation
The best thing about my gran is, she is my gran
And I love her so much.

***Charlotte Thurlby  (8)***
**Church Langton Primary School**

## DAYS OF THE WEEK

Monday is here, I'm off to school
I'm dressed in uniform not so cool.

Tuesday is here, I'm so bored
Hurrah the school team has scored.

Wednesday is here and it's spelling day
Just no time to go and play.

Thursday's here, I have PE
Even worse I have RE

Friday, Friday punishment day
No time at all to play.

Saturday's here, Leicester City I cheer
I don't think they're going to win I fear.

Sunday, Sunday full of cheer
Dad comes for a beer.

*Adam Snart (10)*
**Church Langton Primary School**


## MY GRAN

My gran is as wise as an owl
Her hair is like some tangled up string
Her eyes are like the shimmer of the moonlight
Her face is like a wrinkled old plastic bag
When she walks she is like a duck waddling from side to side
When she sits she is like a bat that has been flying all night
When she laughs she is like a magical fairy flying away to
                a far away land
The best thing about my gran is that she is funny and
Makes me giggle and laugh when I feel sad.

*Larissa Wale (9)*
**Church Langton Primary School**

## CHARGE OF THE HORSE BRIGADE
*(Based on 'The Charge Of The Light Brigade' by Alfred Lord Tennyson)*

Half a neigh, half a neigh,
Half a neigh onward,
All in the valley of tack,
Galloped the six hundred.
Forward the horse brigade,
'Charge for the whips!' he said
Into the valley of tack
Galloped the six hundred.
Forward the horse brigade
Was there a horse dismay'd,
Not tho' the horse knew,
A horse had blunder'd,
Theirs not to make reply,
Theirs not to reason why,
Theirs but to do and cry,
Into the valley of tack
Galloped the six hundred.

*Jade Louise Sharp (10)*
**Church Langton Primary School**

## MY TEACHER

My teacher is a maths wiz.
She sparkles and she shines.
She takes care of the class
And makes sure they write in lines.
She's a really good teacher.
She looks after us so well.
My teacher is so brilliant.
She makes me want to yell!

*Charlotte Alloway (8)*
**Church Langton Primary School**

## DIARY OF THE WEEK

Back to school I'm sad to say
This only means one thing - Monday!

Tuesday's here, we all will learn
To line up and wait our turn.

Wednesday's come I want to cry.
I think Miss Mathews is a spy.

Thursday it's a cross-country run.
Don't like the teacher's idea of fun.

Friday's nearly up I'm glad.
At this time no one is sad.

It's Saturday, I'm finally free
We'll have a great time my friends and me.

It's Sunday and I'm not a sinner
Just off to Gran's for roast dinner.

*Alice Ruggles  (11)*
**Church Langton Primary School**


## THE GREY OWL

As the grey owl glides
Through the night,
His shadow darkens the ground.
His beady eyes flicker upon his prey.
As he dives silently down,
As he drops his pellets,
The mice lie dead.
And as dawn comes,
He makes his way,
Back to his tree.

*Lottie Davies  (9)*
**Church Langton Primary School**

## THE WEEK POEM

Monday's here, I'm off to school.
Once again under teacher's rule.

Tuesday is not the best day of the week.
I think I'll give Sam's ear a tweek.

Wednesday's nearly up.
And still no luck.

Thursday is ok, it's PE.
But it's followed by RE.

Friday's here at last.
Time's going fast.

Saturday and off to the shops.
Off to the butcher's to get some chops.

Sunday's full of cheer.
Dad comes for a beer.

***Laura Jane Freestone (10)***
**Church Langton Primary School**


## UNDER THE SEA

You see dolphins, whales and starfish too
Swimming in the sea so blue.
There are great big rocks under the sea
Where pretty fish live happily.

Fish shimmering, coral bright
Glinting wondrously in the light.
Dolphins are a beautiful sight
For their leathery skin sparkles in the starry nights.

***Hannah Francesca Smith (9)***
**Church Langton Primary School**

## MY GRAN

My gran is as old as a pyramid.
Her hair is like a giant marshmallow that sits on her head.
Her eyes are like the sparkliest of stars.
Her face is like all the elephants' wrinkles in the world.
When she walks she wobbles like a person on huge stilts.
When she sits she is like a weight that doesn't want to move.
When she laughs she is like a happy squeaky toy.
When she sleeps she is like a teddy bear alone on a bed.
The best thing about my gran is she is kind, loving and
brilliant at heart.

*Joseph Currie  (8)*
**Church Langton Primary School**


## GHOST OF THE AIR

The ghost of the forest
Owl, most mysterious
Goes hooting to the moon.

Suddenly the beak snaps
And claws catch.
The rat is dead.
In a peek of sunlight
He hides away until another
Night.

*Elliot McClymont  (8)*
**Church Langton Primary School**

## THE BIRD BRIGADE
*(Based on 'The Charge Of The Light Brigade' by Alfred Lord Tennyson)*

Half a flap, half a flap,
Half a flap onward.
All above the farm.
Flew the six hundred.
Forward the bird brigade,
'Swoop down to the crop,' he said.
Down to the crop
Flew the six hundred

Forward the bird brigade
Was there a bird dismayed?
Not though the flock knew
Some bird had blundered
Into the blazing guns
Into the mouth of hell
All above the farm
Flew the six hundred.

***Georgina Atkinson (11)***
**Church Langton Primary School**


## FOREST GHOST

The forest ghost glides through the night,
The bright stars make it stand out
The forest ghost flying with pure might
For the rats and mice as silent as the night's air.
But the fixed-eyed ghost searches every corner of the night.
Until the sun shines and it hides.
Out of sound and sight.

***Patrick Robertson (8)***
**Church Langton Primary School**

## CHARGE OF THE TEACHERS
*(Based on 'The Charge Of The Light Brigade' by Alfred Lord Tennyson)*

Half a level, half a level
Half a level onward
Into the valley of SATS
Taught the six hundred
'Forward the teacher brigade,
Will you be quiet,' they cried
Into the valley of SATS
Taught the six hundred
Theirs not to make reply
Theirs not to reason why
Theirs but to make reply
Into the valley of SATS
Taught the six hundred
Child to the right of them
Child to the left of them
Whispering and talking
'Well done,' she shouted,
'You've done me proud,'
Out of the valley of SATS
Taught the six hundred.

***Imogen Sloan  (11)***
**Church Langton Primary School**


## SPRING - CINQUAIN

Chicks born,
Flowers emerge,
Lambs bounce in the green fields,
Rustle, bustle, crackle, rattle,
Fresh breeze.

***Imogen Jane Haynes  (9)***
**Church Langton Primary School**

## FAMILY BRIGADE
*(Based on 'The Charge Of The Light Brigade' by Alfred Lord Tennyson)*

Clean your room, clean your room,
Clean your room onward,
Into the house of hell
Strode the child onward.

Mum to the right of her
Dad to the left of her
Into the room of death,
Strode the child onward

**Tammie Smith (10)**
**Church Langton Primary School**


## KILLER OWL

Killer owl
Looking for its prey
Moving swiftly
Swooping down
Like a ghost in the night sky
Talons like knives
Beak like a pothook
And eyes like bullets
What is it?
It's the *killer owl.*

**Kristian Garbett (8)**
**Church Langton Primary School**

# OLD THOMAS TAYLOR

Old Thomas Taylor lives on Green Park Road
He is ninety or more.
Every day he walks to Green Park,
Where the wind ran wild,
Where he used to play,
Years ago,
With his friends on Green Park.
But now he's older he goes there
To remember
His memories.

*George Rhodes (8)*
*Church Langton Primary School*


# MY GRAN

My gran is as small as a child,
Her hair is like tiny white threads,
Her eyes are like glistening dew on wet grass,
Her face is like a scrunched up bit of kitchen roll,
When she walks she is like a bird,
When she sits she is like a small sack of potatoes,
When she laughs she is like a kookaburra that can't stop,
When she sleeps she is like a hibernating animal
The best thing about my gran is she spoils me with
treats and chocolate.

*Amie Lauper-Bull (9)*
*Church Langton Primary School*

## DEER BRIGADE

*(Based on 'The Charge Of The Light Brigade' by Alfred Lord Tennyson)*

Half a leap, half a leap
Half a leap onward
Into the valley of bracken
Bounded the six hundred.

Sprint the deer brigade
Stamped the tigers he said
Not tho' they knew
Someone had blunder'd
Pounces to the left of them
Pounces to the right of them
Pounces in front of them
Into the valley of bracken
Bounded the six hundred.

Half-jawed, half-eaten
Theirs not to run and cry
Theirs not to reason why
Theirs not to do and die
Into the valley of death
Into the jaws of danger
No more, six hundred.

***Alexia Garbett (10)***
**Church Langton Primary School**

## SUNSET

The sunset is beautiful
red, orange, yellow, pink and blue
I sit with my friends
share what I did that day.
The sunset is beautiful
red,
orange,
yellow,
pink,
blue.

I wake up in the morning
open my curtains
sunrise greets me
red,
orange,
yellow,
pink,
blue.

I watch the golden leaves from
my window
swirling, swirling
to the ground
golden, golden,
swirling down.

**Hannah Forsyth (9)**
**Fairfield Preparatory School**

## SUNSET

The sun sets

red
pink
orange
yellow

And rises

yellow
orange
pink
red

The clouds look grey
The buildings seem dark

The background looks like
a fruit bowl of
red strawberries
pink peaches
orange oranges
yellow bananas.

***Imogen Clements  (9)***
**Fairfield Preparatory School**

## SUNSET

The sun rises as I wake,
The bright pink colours shine over a lake.
Puddles glint in the light,
The colours brighten to make a beautiful sight.
Hedgehogs scurry out of their holes,
To find the sun uncovering the moles.

Leaves fall from the trees,
Covering all the flowers not one left for the bees.
The sun feels so warm,
There'll be no need for a storm.
Autumn dawns over our house,
Quiet even, as a mouse.

*Elliott Hefford (9)*
*Fairfield Preparatory School*


## SUNSET

The sun is going down
Deer are going to sleep

The little deer thinks
He should stay up to see
The sunrise

He waits and waits and waits
Just falling to sleep
It comes, sunrise
Purple, orange, pink and yellow

He jumps for joy
'Sunrise,' he says
He runs across the golden leaves.

*Natalie Charlton (9)*
*Fairfield Preparatory School*

# THE SUNSET

As I wake I look out my golden window
And see a happy sun looking at me.
The wind blowing
As the hunt keeps going
And going.
The sky is glowing pink
The sun will disappear in a wink
The sun sinks in the west
The hunters have done their best
The sun goes to bed
The day's over
Evening comes
The little children suck their thumbs
And sleep.

*Harriet Girgis (9)*
*Fairfield Preparatory School*


# SUNSET

Red, orange, yellow
Sunset is a paintbox of colours
Red, orange, yellow
Sunset shows the night is getting near
Red, orange, yellow

The sun is disappearing beneath the trees
Red, orange, yellow
The trees look like big black tall figures
Red, orange, yellow
Red, orange, yellow.

*Sam Collington (9)*
*Fairfield Preparatory School*

## LITTLE RED RIDING HOOD

There once was a girl called Red Riding Hood.
Who went to visit her grandma.
She brought cakes that she baked and lemonade that she made
And biscuits that smelt quite delicious.
Her mother told her to be careful, for wolves are all around.
You can hear them by their terrible loud howling sound.
'Don't worry I will be fine,' said Red Riding Hood every time.
So she went into the woods without a care.
She reached her grandma's house and brushed her hair.
She went in with a smile, as she saw her grandma,
She stayed for quite a while.
Her grandma asked her to come near
As Red Riding Hood's eyes filled with fear.
Red Riding Hood took one step closer
And said to grandma 'I don't want to be a boaster
But your head looks like a toaster
And your ears look all curled and battered.'
The devious wolf felt all flattered.
He liked the idea of her being fatted!
He stared with a glare and grabbed her hair.
But Red Riding Hood screamed 'No!' and bellowed 'Let Go!'
Suddenly grandma burst through the door,
'Good heavens,' she cried in a flurry.
Get out of my house in a hurry.
The wolf disappeared into the night
And she did not put up a fight.

*Holly Boorn (9)*
*Frisby CE Primary School*

## MY TEACHER MR WRIGHT

My teacher Mr Wright
Gives you an awful fright
He picks his nose
And bites at his toes

He drinks Pepsi all day long
And sings this very awful song
He gels his hair up in a spike
And always comes to school riding his bike

His classroom's like a tip
And he has a massive lip
However we're always bright
That is my teacher Mr Wright.

*Emilie Ayres (9)*
*Frisby CE Primary School*


## MY SCHOOL

There's some things in my school that drool
We do not have a swimming pool
The dinners are icky
We're ever so picky
But everything else is cool

Chocolate logs taste very nice
But sometimes I find holes made by mice
We all have different views of school
I suppose I think it's pretty cool.

*Kate Rees (9)*
*Frisby CE Primary School*

## GREEDY GOLDILOCKS

Porridge steaming all warm and fluffy,
Along came Goldilocks nasty and huffy,
Guided inside by the sweet smell,
The rest of the story I struggle to tell,
For it's so terrible, rude and sad,
(And I probably get really mad.)
But she went right inside,
'Umm lovely porridge,' she cried.
The first bowl of porridge was far too hot,
The second she found, was cold in the pot,
The third, however, was just right,
She could eat her porridge all night.
Then she found a lonely chair,
Sitting in the cold, frosty air,
The second chair was alright,
But it would give you a very big fright.
The third one was small and nice,
And there she sat dreaming of mice.
Goldilocks crept up the stairs,
To find the beds of the three bears,
The first one was hard and very bumpy
The second was all soggy and lumpy,
The third, however, was a magnificent sight,
A bed in which she could sleep all night.
The bears returned later that morning,
To find the little girl yawning.
'Oh my word,' the bears did shriek
And pulled back the covers to take a peek.
'Call the police,' the bears did wail.
Poor old Goldilocks is locked in jail.

*Rebecca Lucy Coley  (9)*
*Frisby CE Primary School*

## WHERE DO TEACHERS GO?

Where do teachers go?

Do they go to nightclubs?
Do they stay at home?
Do they have a pint at the pub?
Or do they go to Rome?

Where do teachers go?

Do they ever visit Hell?
Do they go to tea?
Do they spend the night in a cell?
Or do they stay at home and watch TV?

Where do teachers go?

Where do you think teachers go
At 25 past 3?
Or are they just the same as you and me.

*Annabel Blake  (8)*
*Frisby CE Primary School*


## SCHOOL

School is bad
School is good
School smells like mouldy mud

Teachers boring
Teachers rough
Teachers big and very tough

Playground slippy
Playground wet
The playground's dangerous, do you want to bet?

*Hannah Mary Dobson  (10)*
*Frisby CE Primary School*

## JACK AND THE BEANSTALK

Jack's mum said, 'Go sell the cow,'
'But mum,' Jack said, 'I don't know how!'
'Go and find a wealthy man
and stuff him in his poxy van.'
'But mum, I couldn't do that.
That's the work of a dirty rat.'
'Well go sell it, and do it now!'
So Jack traded the cow for a magic bean
And told his mum they're not what they seem,
Then Jack's mum flew into a rage,
And threw them in among the sage,
In the morning Jack saw a beanstalk,
And to the top Jack did walk,
But there was too much hustle,
And way too much bustle,
So Jack climbed back down,
And saw the whole town,
Had some sort of huge replacement,
With a big repulsive basement,
With anger Jack cried out loud,
'Why now!' he yelled, 'Why now!'
And so he jumped into the air,
In hope that someone would declare,
That the old town would reappear
And under eighteens were allowed some beer,
But Jack's wish did not come true,
(This is just between me and you)
Then after he lived in a faraway land
With dwarfs and fairies and heaps of sand.

*Chloe Louise Kutkus Morton (9)*
*Frisby CE Primary School*

## BROTHERS

I have an annoying little brother
I wish like others I had another
Can I get one from the town
Or do I have to dig right down?
Can I get one on the market
Or do they sell them in the Antarctic?
Can I get one at the toy shop?
If they're on the mountains, I'll climb to the top
It all seems like lots of bother
I think instead I'll ask my mother.

*Amber Batten  (8)*
*Frisby CE Primary School*


## MY DOG

I like my dog and he likes me,
We have fun in the sea.

We eat hot dogs and run along the sand,
I give him treats from my hand.

We play catch and football too,
He likes chewing my favourite shoe.

I like my dog and he likes me,
Without my dog where would I be?

*Jack Swallow  (9)*
*Frisby CE Primary School*

## CLASS FOUR

Class Four are so poor
They don't use doors
They are so weird
They all have beards
The school goes *pop*
When people flop

They don't do work
They act like jerks
They weirdest one is called Drew
Who cries alone on the loo
They are all so dumb
The teacher never lets us have good fun

Class Four are so cool
They always jump into the swimming pool
They never read books
They are rubbish cooks
Class Four I'm afraid that's us.

*Sam Parker (10)*
*Frisby CE Primary School*


## CHRISTMAS

C   rackers going bang
H   olly on the table tops
R   udolf with his nose so bright
I    vy decorating the rooms at night
S   now gently falling
T   urkey being roasted in the cookery
M  istletoe hanging low
A   ngels singing clearly
S   anta's on his sleigh.

*Charlotte Griffin (9)*
*Frisby CE Primary School*

## THE THREE BEARS

The three bears went out for a stroll,
After putting their porridge into the bowl.
Then along came Goldilocks,
Wearing her special party socks.
When she found the first bowl of porridge,
She found it tasted rather horrid.
But when she tried the second one,
She held her nose 'cause of the pong.
When she tried the next bowl of oats,
'Wow this is good,' she did loudly gloat.
Then she sat down on a chair,
The one in the corner over there.
*My, this is too hard*, she thought to herself,
*I'd much rather go and sit on a shelf.*
The second chair was terribly soft,
'What a horrible chair,' the little girl scoffed.
The next chair she saw, was a dear little thing,
But it broke when she sat on it, with a crack and a ping.
'Oh dear, oh dear, oh dear,' she said,
'I really want to go to bed.'
So she crept up the stairs,
To find the beds of the three bears.
The first bed was rather too big
And it smelt quite awfully like a pig!
The next bed was just the right size,
But Goldilocks found it was full of flies.
The last bed was just right,
She could've slept there peacefully all night,
When the bears came back, they had a fright,
But they ate her up in one big bite.

*Katherine Rabey  (8)*
**Frisby CE Primary School**

## THE THREE LITTLE PIGS

The wolf appeared at a little door,
Like the house, it was made of straw,
A little pig inside,
'It's the wolf,' he cried.
The wolf outside heard this call,
'I'll eat him up bones and all,'
So he blew down the door,
Made entirely of straw,
So that was the end of a pig.
The one wearing a giant wig

Soon the wolf followed a trail of bricks
And found a house made of sticks.
The little pig had just finished school,
'Mmm another one,' the wolf drooled,
But the pig realised he was being watched
And drew a gun already cocked,
But the wolf suspecting danger,
Ate up the unsuspecting stranger,
So the end of pig number two,
The one coloured entirely blue.

Pig number three heard a warning shout,
A handful of curses did he spout,
The wolf heard these words and hurried by,
Only to be turned into a giant wolf pie.
Then from his tummy came a shout,
'Let us out and end this bout,'
So he opened up Wolf's poor tum,
And rescued his two piggy chums,
That's the tale of three little pigs,
Who ate a wolf so bad and big.

*Stephen Tatlow  (9)*
*Frisby CE Primary School*

## THE TROLL AND THE ROLLS

There once was a bridge guarded by a troll.
He just sat there eating a peanut butter roll.
Many have tried to get across
The old dirty bridge covered in moss.
But all of them have failed,
Thinking, *That horrible fat troll should be jailed!*
Along came three goats one day.
To get across they thought you had to pay.
Because the grass was so green,
Then they noticed the troll that was mean.
The three goats,
Saw some boats.
They all jumped in,
But the motors wouldn't begin.
So they climbed out
And began to shout . . .
'We'll give you all the peanut butter rolls you can eat,
If you let us past because it's really quite neat.'
So the troll agreed
And got all the rolls he would need.
So the lovely green grass the goats did now own.
They let everyone in, so no one would moan.

*Hope Greig  (10)*
**Frisby CE Primary School**


## MY DOG MAX

My dog Max is as dark as the dark night
He is so fast that he can only see a blur when he is running
He is so playful that in the middle of the night
He wakes me up to play
I love my dog Max.

*Aimee Odendaal  (10)*
**Newbold CE Primary School**

## THE LITTLE MONSTER

Tiny feet,
Millimetre claws,
Needle teeth.

Low belly,
Spotty chest,
Loud haired tail.

Loud barks,
Zig- zag runs,
Black, tan, white.

Black, tan, white,
Black, tan, white,
But I love Daisy!

*Kendall McEwan (10)*
*Newbold CE Primary School*


## ANIMALS I LIKE

Horses are furry
Pigs are dirty
Dogs are cute
Cats are curly
Mice are fast
Birds are peckish
Guinea pigs are hairy
Ducks are quackers
Chickens are clucky
Monkeys are silly
Ferrets are playful
But best of all as far as I can see
Is the lovely, friendly donkey.

*Joanna Emily Louise Peat (8)*
*Newbold CE Primary School*

## DREAMS

My feelings as I wake are.
The most tingling things.
The stars,
The sun,
A brilliant time.
I get up and get dressed.
As if I have the world to myself.
Bliss,
Dreams,
And a big, enormous fantasy!
I look around and think.
What shall I do?
Walk,
Think,
Or dream and go back to sleep.

*Sean Peat (10)*
**Newbold CE Primary School**


## FRIENDS

My friend is kind to me
Because she listens.
My friend shares her things with me
When I am at her house.
My friend helps me do my work
When I am stuck.
My friend plays with me
When I am sad
*My bestest friend ever!*

*Carys Gidlow (8)*
**Newbold CE Primary School**

## SPELLING TEST

There is a spelling test today
Boys and girls compete
But when it comes to the word
They start to turn up the heat.

And the teacher says, 'Spell - girl,'
The children write it on their sheet
All the girls themselves got it wrong
Next the teacher says, 'bleat.'

All the boys laugh but still get it wrong
All the words that followed 'crest and breast'
And at the end, oh what a mess
The boys got them wrong, except all the rest.

They didn't do the spelling test at all!

***Michael Mannion  (10)***
*Newbold CE Primary School*


## MYSTERY PET

Curled up in a basket.
Plays with a ball.
Sometimes not very tall.
They need love and attention.
Prancing and dancing.
Howling at night
What am I?
I'm a dog.

***Nancy Ella Waldrum  (8)***
*Newbold CE Primary School*

## MY FLUFFY PET

I have a pet
I leave it to set
How can it be when my cat leaves me?
I feed it
I breed it
I give it TLC
My cat loves fuss on my knee
I play with him when he plays fair
Then I do care
His name is Snowie
When I look at him
I dream of snowflakes
Falling as soft as clouds.

*Sian Summerfield  (9)*
*Newbold CE Primary School*


## RUGBY

Big, bulky people
Tape rapped round their heads
Sludgy pitches
Muddy legs
Cauliflower-ears full of blood
Kicking each other with their studs.
*Rugby's great!*

*Thomas Bale  (9)*
*Newbold CE Primary School*

## JAMES BOND

*Bang, bang* I'm dead,
James Bond shot me dead,
I shot him in the nose,
And it bled like a hose.
He uses a PP7,
A gun with a deadly heaven,
The best thing about 007,
Is he sends people to Heaven.
James Bond is the best,
His bullets are like lemon zest,
Whatever you do,
Don't try and rest,
Because his aiming is truly the best.

**Harry Miles  (9)**
*Newbold CE Primary School*


## HONEY THE HORSE

Her shining coat is like the rain
Her ears are soldiers standing to attention
Her white mane ripples in the wind
Her golden body is as bright as the sun
Her white tail flowing like water
Her golden neck arched high and proud
Her tail swishes away the flies

She's galloping through the field
Faster and faster, on and on
She pauses for a second
Catches her breath
Then off again

**Jessica Fardoe  (10)**
*Newbold CE Primary School*

## CONSOLES

PS2s are wonders,
Better than any Gameboy.
Who'da thought one box
Could bring us so much joy.

Gamecubes are techno wonders,
From games on Earth and Mars.
To the best agent 007,
And the wars above the stars.

PS1's old school,
With bounty hunters galore.
But you'll need to play the games
To find out what's in store . . .

***Thomas David Renton  (11)***
*Newbold CE Primary School*


## WATER

Water is smooth
like a summer's
breeze.
Flowing its gentle
way.
Flowing smooth
flowing calm
flowing
always
flowing.

***Stefan Beniston  (10)***
*Newbold CE Primary School*

## KILLING MACHINE

It roars like thunder
Fast as lightning
Running through the meadow
Perfect killing machine.

Its black stripes like lightning bolts
Bloodstained teeth and hideous claws
It runs like the wind
And leaps through the air.

It stares at its prey through the long grass
Then tries to pounce on it
Then, then the chase begins
But the tiger wins.

*Rhiannon Winlow  (10)*
*Newbold CE Primary School*


## A FANTASY ISLAND OF INK

In the fantasy Island of Ink
huge trees grow the colour pink.
Birds are huge and fly around with their massive wings.
They have a massive beach with sand,
it is really grand
and there is a place called Mountain Land
full of mountains, birds, trees and sand.
The primitive people live in mud huts
They live on fish with fruits and nuts
The starfish they eat is really sweet
but it's not exactly a lovely treat
Now my grand tour is done
I hope you have fun
In the fantasy Island of Ink.

*Katie Hutchinson  (10)*
*Newcroft CP School*

# A SWEET POEM

I dream to live on a land sweets,
rivers of chocolate, a tasty treat!
Icing grass ground
and candyfloss clouds!

Houses of gingerbread,
sweet candy bed!
Cushions of marshmallow,
toffee curtains that hang low!

Caramel rain,
marzipan frost on the lane!
Ice cream snow,
a sun, a boiled sweet, with its round glow!

Candy mountains across the land,
sherbert instead of the golden sand!
A lively sea of fizzy pop,
a lime jelly forest with sprinkles on top!

The thing I like about this dreamland,
is that you can eat anything,
that comes in your hand!

*Neha Puntambekar (10)*
*Newcroft CP School*

# BONFIRE NIGHT

The first firework is at the ready,
Lucy is clutching her pink fluffy teddy.

With a whizz and a boom,
Off goes a rocket heading straight for home!

Spinning, spinning, never to stop,
The Catherine wheels are like spinning tops.

Up and down goes the Roman candle,
Its flames are always in a tangle.

Next comes the flowerpot,
Red, orange, purple and pink.

The crackling thunder lights up the sky,
Boy, how it flies.

*Ellie Bennett  (8)*
*Newcroft CP School*


# MY LITTLE SISTERS

Little sisters I have two,
One is four and the other quite new,
By new I mean she's half a year,
She is very cute, cuddly and dear,
But dinner time is not much fun,
When she starts eating it's best to run,
The middle sis, the one who's four,
Who's always knocking at my bedroom door,
Who won't give me ten minute's break,
And all I think is *for goodness sake,*
But I do love them, my sisters two,
Though I don't always show it, I really do.

*Charlotte Woods  (10)*
*Newcroft CP School*

## SOOTY MY BUNNY

I have a little bunny
he lives out in his hutch
he really likes to come inside
and have a lot of fuss.
He likes to run around me
and nibble at my hair
he hops and jumps and follows me
almost everywhere.
He is a lovely bunny
I love him very much
I couldn't be without him now
I'd miss him way too much.

*Kerry Exon  (10)*
*Newcroft CP School*


## MY PET, HONEY

I have got a hamster.
Honey is her name.
She plays in the night
And sleeps in the day.
She likes to be stroked
And she wouldn't bite you.
She runs around in her ball
And tries hiding from you.
Honey's very fluffy
And also very cute.
With her long, creamy hair,
So soft and silky.
She really is number one.

*Jade Beedham  (9)*
*Newcroft CP School*

## SCHOOL

Geography, history
English and maths
Merit badges, points
But the bathrooms
Don't have baths

Does anyone like school
Or do they think it's a bore?
I like Newcroft School
And that's for sure

Pencils, rubbers
Sharpeners and pens
Can anyone let me into a secret and
Tell me they have a secret den?
But I want to know whether
Teachers like school or
Do they think it is a real bore?

*Beth Wright (10)*
*Newcroft CP School*

# WET

Wet, wet
I'm really wet
Splashing in the puddles
Getting wet

Wet, wet
I'm really wet
Splashing in the sea waves
Getting wet

Wet, wet
I'm really wet
Splashing in the paddling pool
Getting wet

Now I'm . . .
Wet.

*Rachael Burton  (9)*
**Newcroft CP School**


# THE DINOSAURS

D   inosaur was a scary beast
I   n the long years past.
N   ibbling grass or eating meat
O   thers ran very fast.
S   ome of them were very big
A   ll of them now dead.
U   nderground their bones are found,
R   eally scary, some with wings,
S   caly skin and a spiky head.

*Cameron Hirons  (9)*
**Newton Burgoland Primary School**

## LISTEN

Listen!
What can you hear?
The chirping of the birds singing out loud,
The laughing of the children playing in a crowd.

Look!
What can you see?
The children swinging to and fro from the climbing frame,
Playing a silly game.

Touch!
What can you feel?
The grass tickling your cold feet,
We can't wait to feel the summer heat.

Sniff!
What can you smell?
The swamp pondweed blowing through the air,
The sweet smell of grass everywhere.

Listen!
What can you hear?
The squeaking of the swings going up and down, side to side,
The children whizzing down the slippery slide.

*Bethan Jacka (8)*
*Newton Burgoland Primary School*

## LISTEN

Listen!
What can you hear?
Children laughing while they play on the park,
Their mum calling them in before it gets dark.

Look!
What can you see?
The swing swaying from side to side,
Children playing on the slide.

Touch!
What can you feel?
Feel the rubber of the 'watz' seat,
As the ground spins under your feet.

Sniff!
What can you smell?
Smell the flowers growing in the sun,
Under the tree where the rabbits run.

Listen!
What can you hear?
Creaking, shouting, crying,
All the sounds of the playground.

*Sara Green  (8)*
*Newton Burgoland Primary School*

## LISTEN

Listen!
What can you hear?
The creaking of the swings going up and down,
The squealing of a boy, acting a clown.

Look!
What can you see?
The children whizzing round on the roundabout,
See them swinging in and out.

Touch!
What can you feel?
The waving breeze blowing on your cold hands,
The safe tarmac that feels like sand.

Sniff!
What can you smell?
The freshness of the spring grass growing,
A man on his tractor mowing.

Listen!
What can you hear?
The whistling around the trees,
I hear the buzzing of the bees.

*Hannah Barnes (9)*
*Newton Burgoland Primary School*

## LISTEN

Listen!
What can you hear?
The children screaming in the playground
The roundabout creaking as it spins around

Listen!
What can you hear?
The jingle of the chains on the swings
Swaying up and down
The squelching of the children
Running in the mud

Listen!
What can you hear?
Listen!
Just listen
What do you hear?
Everything in the playground.

*Joshua Carr  (7)*
*Newton Burgoland Primary School*


## MY SCHOOL IS THE BEST

S   chool is for learning and for play.
C   oming here very day.
H   istory, maths and science too.
O   r maybe geography's best for you.
O   utside playtime with our mates.
L   aughing, playing, skipping and skates.

*Carl Baillie  (10)*
*Newton Burgoland Primary School*

## LISTEN

Listen!
What can you hear?
The wind swaying around in the air,
Leaves blowing around everywhere.

Listen!
What can you hear?
The children laughing as they play along,
Singing a funny song.

Listen!
What can you hear?
Bees buzzing collecting nectar from flowers,
They go on for hours and hours.

***Rameeka Banning  (8)***
*Newton Burgoland Primary School*


## LISTEN

Listen
What can you hear?
The children screaming and singing loud
On the roundabout whizzing round.

Listen
What can you hear?
Children throwing rocks in the swamp
*Splash, splash*, as the rocks hit the water.

Sniff
What can you smell?
The smelly swamp weed
In the slimy green water.

***Drew Fores  (7)***
*Newton Burgoland Primary School*

## THE FROZEN MAN

Down by the frozen pond
In the corner of the village
Trees crack their icy fingers
When the wind hits them.
The bull's breath – slipping away like frosty clouds.
The grass – stiff and shiny
When the moon sparkles on it.
Hedges and trees
Looking like big icy boulders
Standing still.
And the tumble-down farmhouse
Trapped in the cold, gloomy mist.
A man is walking slowly
So slowly.
The grass sounding
*Crunch*
*Crunch*
As the man steps on.
The man
Stumbling through the blizzard
Towards houses.
The gloomy street light
Showing the man's shadow.
But back in my warm, cosy house
The fire is burning
Red, yellow and gold.
The warmth permeates the house.
I see this frozen man.
Come in
Come in.

***Glynn Ruddock (11)***
**Newton Burgoland Primary School**

## LISTEN

Listen
What can you hear?
The children screaming and
Playing in the park.
The woof of the dog
Beginning to bark

Look
What can you see?
The mini roundabout twirling around

Sniff
What can you smell?
The awful smell of pondweed.

Touch
What can you feel?
The wind blowing against your face.

*Daniel White (9)*
**Newton Burgoland Primary School**

## THE COLD BLAST

Cold
Cold
In the centre of the village
Are the frozen, shadowy trees
Crying for warmth
All alone
Alone
Alone.
The bushes
Flapping stiffly
In the chill strong breeze
The roof tiles
Surrounded by the blasts of icy wind
Crying
Crying
Crying
Oh! To be warm!

*Liam Reeves  (11)*
**Newton Burgoland Primary School**

## THE ICY CHILD

Far, far away on the outskirts of the village
In the forest
The scary phantoms haunt
Trees and bushes join them
Paths are cloudy
Misty and
Crunchy
Grass is stiff and frozen
There is a small girl
Her hands and her feet are so cold
So odd
In the biting chill
She is holding on for dear life
Just one minute longer
Just one minute longer
Hoping
Praying
Here in my house it is snug and cosy
My cat is so warm and cuddly
Sitting by the fire
The fire
Blazing blue, purple and gold
Come in my child
Come in.

*Hannah Robinson  (10)*
*Newton Burgoland Primary School*

## WINTER EVENINGS

The dark shadowy trees
Looking threatening, threatening
The ice-covered ponds
Ice as thick as tractor tyres
The signpost
Rocking and waving
With icicles
Hanging like frostbitten fingers
The grass glistens frostily in the moonlight
The chilly wind soaring through the treetops
The fox breathes a cloud of ice
The gate ceases swinging
As the ice freezes the hinges
An elderly man shuffles along the
Frozen path
Trying to reach his destination
Moving slower
Ever slower
His breath turns into a misty cloud of ice
He's desperate to get home
Here in my warm and snug home
The cat purrs in front of the fire
Glad to be inside
The clock ticks and ticks
The stranger approaches
I welcome him in
Come in
Come in
Come in.

*Edward Storer  (11)*
**Newton Burgoland Primary School**

## ICY DAYS

Frosty roads
Frosty cars
Frosty pavements
Frosty drives
Legs cold
Legs shiver
Legs chilly
Cold
Cold
Cold
Soft pillow
Soft bed
Soft quilt
Rest your head.

*Ryan Ruddock  (9)*
*Newton Burgoland Primary School*


## A WINTER'S SCENE

Far, far
Out at the edge of the town
The frozen trees crack.
Twigs fall off.
Stiff hedges stand still like soldiers.
In the moonlight
Badgers hide in their setts
Trying to keep warm.
Owls
Searching for food
On the frozen, tar-blackened road.
The grass
Sparkling like diamonds in the timeless air.

*Tony Watts  (10)*
*Newton Burgoland Primary School*

# A WINTER'S NIGHT

A winter's night - on the outskirts of the village
The icy wind is blowing the branches of the spooky, moonlit trees.
White frost on the moonlight
The grass
Frosted and sparkling
The grass crunching as the fox walks across.
Cars on their drives
Covered in frost.
The frosted fences stand like guards near their gate posts.
Fences covered in the ice-cold frost.
A man is walking
Along the coal black road
All alone
All alone
His nose red
As the wind whips his face.
Trudging along so slowly,
So slowly.
Me
Inside my snug, cosy home
Sitting by the warm, blazing fire
Its colours of gold, orange,
Red and yellow.
The fire
Spreading warmth and comfort
Throughout the house.
When the man comes to my house
I'll let him in
Let him in
Let him in.

*Matthew Jacka (10)*
**Newton Burgoland Primary School**

59

## A WINTER'S SCENE

Enter
Enter the deep, white, frozen village.
The twigs on the trees
Snapping
As the howling winds slam against their white, shadowy branches.
An owl
Hooting in the cold wind
As a frosty gate squeaks - being forced open
As the wind batters against it.
The glistening pond shimmers in the moonlight
As the frost hits the ground.
A child is shivering
As he plods
Through the crispy, crunching frost of the winter's night.
Walking
Walking
Walking.

*Laura Green  (10)*
*Newton Burgoland Primary School*


## THE BONFIRE

This cloud of smoke in other hours,
Was leaves and grass, green twigs and flowers.

This bitter-sweet dead that blows along,
Was once a breathing of a rose.

This smell of you, takes a breath down my spine,
With daffodils on ladybirds.

This is the end, not quite, far,
Over the hills, and over the mills.

*Maneet Sagoo  (10)*
*Normanton-on-Soar Primary School*

## AUTUMN'S MAIDEN

Autumn's maiden is here,
With her veil of night and crown of crop,
Her gown is woven of water that has stopped like ice.

Summer roses fall on her,
White dew forms like pearls around her neck.

Her lips open,
They sing a song,
They sing a song of bright, bright red apples,
They sing a song of dark, dark long nights.

Summer roses fall on her,
White dew forms like pearls around her neck.

As the maiden walks,
Her hair, her golden brown hair falls to the ground,
Falls to the ground like leaves in a breeze,
Like leaves in a breeze they are lifted up again,
As she turns her wilting, beautiful face towards the winter queen
All the animals run away.

Autumn's maiden is here!

*Jennifer Harrison  (11)*
*Normanton-on-Soar Primary School*


## PEACE

Why in this world do we have to fight?
This pushing and shoving, it's not a nice sight.
We are all the same, black or white,
But this racism it's just not right.
We all have a heart and we all have a brain.
So all this fight has got to *stop!*

*Kyle Carlisle-Sankey  (10)*
*Normanton-on-Soar Primary School*

## FREE

Why does there have to be racism?
Why can't we just be free?
Why do we have to fight?
Why does it have to be?

Just because we're different colours,
It shouldn't cause a fight.
Why can't we just play together?
Coloured or white.

Let's put a stop to racism,
We can if we work as a team.
It shouldn't really be in the world,
So let everybody be *free!*

***Matthew Hawes  (9)***
***Normanton-on-Soar Primary School***


## YES!

I see the player
I see the ball
With my new boots I win the ball
I run up the field
And have a shot
It breaks the net
And rebounds back
The crowd cheers
So I run to them
I cheer myself
I shout '*Yes!*'

***James Wilks  (10)***
***Normanton-on-Soar Primary School***

## THE GHOST

The white sheet walks solemnly over the dull, dull sky
Witch hugs the village, it waves a chill.
The white stranger who haunts our village
With a sheet all silvery white.
Who is he?
Who keeps us locked up all day?

Who, why?

Has a man so full of evil
Has he got no heart?
Does he shiver at the howl of a wolf?
Who make this man so dark?
Who can help him?

Two weeks later, the cold chill, white man
Still roams the creepy sky
But!

The man has changed, he is the *ghost, ghost, ghost.*

*Joe Toon  (10)*
**Normanton-on-Soar Primary School**


## DREAMS

Clouds floating in my head,
As I lie still with my eyes closed, in my cosy bed,
Floating, floating past the London Eye,
Pyramids and the hideous Minoutaur.

I touch a dream I know it's there,
I see it drifting in the air,
I see a figure faraway,
Drifting to the light of day.

*Francesca Hibbins  (9)*
**Normanton-on-Soar Primary School**

## FLAMBOROUGH FAIR

Fluffy clouds form patterns in the air
Watching grandmas and granddads sit in their chair,
People are happy everywhere
While we go to Flamborough fair.

Children are watching everywhere
While birds fly in the air,
We hope the sun is there
While we go to Flamborough fair.

Rushing, rushing for the rides,
There's a wheel lets go for a ride,
Children are happy everywhere
While we are at Flamborough fair.

*Cathryn Brain  (10)*
*Normanton-on-Soar Primary School*


## GIVE IN

Give in, give in, we will find you,
Stop it, stop it, give in now.
We will find you, give in, give in,
Stop that now!
Stop it, stop it, now or else,
Someone will find you.
Give that child back now or else,
Don't make a move or we will
Find you.

You can run but you can't hide!

*Paul Johnson  (10)*
*Normanton-on-Soar Primary School*

## AN AUTUMN TALE

As leaves wilt then fall with no sound
Colours of yellow and brown lie on the ground.
Nights draw in, that's a fact,
You will even need a scarf and hat.
Autumn has begun.
Conkers drop as they ripen.
As weather changes hot to cold,
Out with the new, in with the old.
Animals scurry around as they gather their food
Summer has finished and that's bad news.

*Danielle Evans (11)*
*Normanton-on-Soar Primary School*


## THINK

Think before you do something.
Think about the things you say.
Think of others before yourself.
Think about someone's feelings,
              and help make their day.
*So think.*

*Christopher Hellier (9)*
*Normanton-on-Soar Primary School*


## WINTER

The snow is falling all around,
White snowflakes fall silently to the ground,
Snowmen, snowballs, lots of fun,
Have a look what winter has done.

*Holly Bishop (10)*
*Normanton-on-Soar Primary School*

## TEN BABY ALIENS

*Ten* baby aliens in their ship,
One paid a fine, then there were
Nine.

*Nine* baby aliens in their ship,
One became bait, then there were
Eight.

*Eight* baby aliens in their ship,
One went to Heaven, then there were
Seven.

*Seven* baby aliens in their ship,
One ate some sticks, then there were
Six.

*Six* baby aliens in their ship,
One took a dive, then there were
Five.

*Five* baby aliens in their ship,
One broke the door, then there were
Four.

*Four* baby aliens in their ship,
One hit a bee, then there were
Three.

*Three* baby aliens in their ship,
One at the loo, then there were
Two.

*Two* baby aliens in their ship,
One found a bomb, then there was
One.

*One* baby alien in his ship,
He was a hero, then there was
Zero!

**Adrian Cox (9)**
**Orchard Community Primary School**


## SPORT 2003

Lennox Lewis the strongest man
Dwain Chambers catch him if you can,
David Beckham scoring kicks
Michael Vaughn is hitting a six.

Baseball hit it out of the ground
American football, a touch down,
Phil Taylor scores treble twenty
Jonathan Edwards jumping metres of plenty.

Australia are on your case
Ian Thorpe is setting the pace,
Steven Hendry pots the black
Tiger's caddy is getting the sack.

Karate men doing high kicks
New Zealand 3, England 6,
Tim Henman wins the set
Paula Radcliffe is dripping with sweat.

**Jack Brownett (10)**
**Orchard Community Primary School**

## MY PUP

My pup, my pup, see her run,
Over the hills into the sun.
Drop down, go to sleep,
Listen closely, hear a weep.
Hardly ever on the ground,
Never gives you a nasty frown.
My pup's a lot of fun,
My pup is after a bun.
Never ever misses a puddle,
Every day after a cuddle.
My pup, my pup, sometimes bad,
My pup, my pup, gets Mum mad.

*Katie Rebecca Lewis (9)*
*Orchard Community Primary School*


## JANUARY'S CHILD IS PLENTY OF TROUBLE

January's child is plenty of trouble,
February's child is stuck in a bubble.
March's child is solving a case,
April's child has a zit on her face.
May's child keeps picking her nose,
June's child is sucking his toes.
July's child has blown a fuse,
August's child keeps singing the blues.
September's child owns a pig,
October's child wears a wig.
November's child wears an itchy vest,
December's child is worse than the rest.

*Harriet Brown (10)*
*Orchard Community Primary School*

## THE ALIEN WHO CAME TO EARTH

There was an alien who got a job,
He was a builder whose name was Bob.
Bob really had some great tools
And he made the others look like fools.
The alien was really bright,
But he could not tell his left from his right.

He was not strong, but very weak,
And every day he ate a leek.
Bob loved to watch television,
He played for Leicester in the first division.
Bob knew French really well,
But boy did he have a funny smell!

Rather suspicious the others got,
Because he won four games on the trot.
He had bright eyes like a cat,
And was not slim, but very fat.
He had quite wrinkly skin,
And always put his rubbish in the bin.

One day his mates went to his house,
They saw a spaceship shaped like a mouse.
All of a sudden the house went dark,
There stood an alien called Jonathan Clark.
In one second there was a rumble,
And they took off to planet Kerjumble.

*Dane Barwell (9)*
*Orchard Community Primary School*

## I LIKE . . .

I like chips but I don't like fish.
I like mugs but I don't like cups.
I like balls but I don't like bats.
I like socks but I don't like pants.
I like cats but I don't like dogs.
I like jumpers but I don't like T-shirts.
I like hardbacks but I don't like paperbacks.
I like cars but I don't like motorbikes.
I like tea but I don't like coffee.
I like paper but I don't like cardboard.
I like DVDs but I don't like videos
I like shoes but I don't like sandals
I like tables but I don't like chairs
I like clocks but I don't like watches
I like you but do you like me?

*Oliver James Tarpey (9)*
*Orchard Community Primary School*


## FOOTBALL

F   rank is a whiz kid at scoring goals,
O   liver's shorts are full of holes.
O   livia's a keeper you just can't bare,
T   homas turns up in red underwear.
B   en is reserve for every league game,
A   dam's shot is poor at aim.
L   iam's a massive United fan,
L   ouis is Henry but without the tan.

*Matthew Cox (10)*
*Orchard Community Primary School*

## SPOOKY HOUSE

Up, up and upon the hills,
You'll never guess what's there,
The spooky house, the spooky house,
That is what's there.

There are hiding witches,
There are terrible ghouls.
There are floating ghosts,
In the spooky house.

When they are disturbed, disturbed,
In the spooky house.
They howl
They growl.
They work as a team,
To make you scream.

The pans go *bash,*
The doors go *slam.*
The hinges always creak,
In the spooky house.

By now I bet you wouldn't dare,
Wouldn't dare to go.
But if you do I warn you,
You'll be in for a scream.

***Sarah-Jane Louise Doherty  (10)***
***Orchard Community Primary School***

## TEN HAPPY SQUIRRELS

Ten happy squirrels, standing by a mine.
One fell down, so then there were nine.

Nine happy squirrels, deciding a fate.
One came true, so then there were eight.

Eight happy squirrels, thinking of Devon.
One went off, so then there were seven.

Seven happy squirrels, eating a Twix.
One went and choked, so then there were six.

Six happy squirrels, feeling alive.
One got shot, so then there were five.

Five happy squirrels, sitting by a door.
One got squashed, so then there were four.

Four happy squirrels, giving a fee.
One wouldn't pay, so then there were three.

Three happy squirrels, playing guess who.
One kept on playing, so then there were two.

Two happy squirrels, lying in the sun.
One got burnt, so then there was one.

One happy squirrel, having a thought.
He fell asleep, so then there were nought.

*Thomas Goodge (9)*
*Orchard Community Primary School*

## THE NAUGHTIEST CLASS EVER

The naughtiest class ever,
Are they clever? No never!

Josh is rocking on the chair,
Ryan's jumping in the air.
Callum's rolling on the floor,
Jake is shouting more and more.

James is screaming in the hall,
George is climbing up the wall.
Adam's blocking up the loo,
Carl is pushing in a queue.

Edward's breaking out of school,
John is drooling, drool, drool, drool.
Ceara's smashing toys up, *crash,*
Mike is running, dash, dash, dash.

Tom is breaking the PC,
Dan's in the loo, wee, wee, wee.
Al's throwing apples around,
A twit smacks on the ground.

The naughtiest class ever,
Are they clever? No, never!

*Edward Foweather  (9)*
**Orchard Community Primary School**

## TEN LITTLE WORMS

Ten little worms,
All in a line.
One went to Nottingham,
And then there were nine.

Nine little worms,
All in a line.
One went to a gate,
And then there were eight.

Eight little worms,
All in a line.
One went to Heaven,
And then there were seven.

Seven little worms,
All in a line.
One went to pick up some sticks,
And then there were six.

Six little worms,
All in a line.
One went in a hive,
And then there were five.

Five little worms,
All in a line.
One went through a door,
And then there were four.

Four little worms,
All in a line.
One climbed a tree,
And then there were three.

Three little worms,
All in a line.
One fell down the loo,
And then there were two.

Two little worms,
All in a line.
One bought a bomb,
And then there was one.

One little worm,
Alone in a line.
He was gone,
Now there is none.

*Steven Kirton  (10)*
*Orchard Community Primary School*


## THE FOOTBALL POEM

Zinadine Zidane doing all the skills
Who plays for Leeds United and England? It's Danny Mills.
David Beckham doing all the free kicks
Ronaldo running as quick.

Roberto Carlos doing all the tackling
Rivaldo doing all the attacking
Michael Owen doing all the scoring
Yeovil Town doing all yawning.

Rio Ferdinand doing all the defending
Marc Overmars doing all the midfielding
Matt Jansen being in a car crash
West Ham lost to Manchester United, wasn't that a thrash.

Mark Draper plays centre
Sol Campbell going to the eagle centre
Most Arsenal players are French
Francis Jeffers is always on the on the bench
One more thing
Come on you England.

*Matthew Rolley  (9)*
*Orchard Community Primary School*

## TEN HAPPY DUCKS

Ten happy ducks,
Swimming in a pond.
One went off,
And became James Bond.

Nine happy ducks,
Swimming in a pond.
One went off,
And had a date.

Eight happy ducks,
Swimming in a pond.
One went off,
And went to Heaven.

Seven happy ducks,
Swimming in a pond.
One went off,
And had a Twix.

Six happy ducks,
Swimming in a pond.
One went off,
And did a dive.

Five happy ducks,
Swimming in a pond.
One went off,
And banged into a door.

Four happy ducks,
Swimming in a pond.
One went off,
Into a tree.

Three happy ducks,
Swimming in a pond.
One went off,
To the zoo.

Two happy ducks,
Swimming in a pond.
One went off,
And had suddenly gone.

One happy duck,
Swimming in a pond.
One went off,
And had a bun.
Then there were none.

*Joshua-Thomas Wilkinson  (9)*
**Orchard Community Primary School**


## TEACHERS

T   all ones,
E   njoyable ones,
A   dmirable ones,
C   areless ones,
H   azardous ones,
E   nergetic ones,
R   easonable ones,
S   tressful ones.

Mine is the *best!*

*Jake Barker  (10)*
**Orchard Community Primary School**

# TEN SILLY FISH

Ten silly fish,
Swimming in the sea.
One did a crime.
Then there were nine.

Nine silly fish,
Swimming in the sea.
One caught a line,
Then there were eight.

Eight silly fish,
Swimming in the sea.
One got shot,
Then there were seven.

Seven silly fish,
Swimming in the sea.
One was shocked,
Then there were six.

Six silly fish,
Swimming in the sea.
One got eaten,
Then there were five.

Five silly fish,
Swimming in the sea.
One went to a shop,
Then there were four.

Four silly fish,
Swimming in the sea.
One went on a ship,
Then there were three.

Three silly fish,
Swimming in the sea.
One went on holiday today,
Then there were two.

Two silly fish,
Swimming in the sea.
One went on a spaceship,
Then there was one.

One silly fish,
Swimming in the sea.
She went to a feast,
Then there was none.

*Guy Williams (9)*
*Orchard Community Primary School*


# THE SEA DOG

Sea dog is sleeping,
Sea dog is snoring,
Sea dog is snooping under the sun.

Finally sea dog wakes up.
Sea dog's running round the trees,
Sea dog's chewing up his toys.
Sea dog's ripping up the leaves,
And Sea dog's scratching at the post.

Sea dog's panting like mad,
Sea dog's getting tired.
And when Sea dog's owner comes out
With his lead,
Sea dog drops to the ground.

*Bethany Ann Homer (9)*
*Orchard Community Primary School*

## TEN BUSY BUZZY BEES

Ten busy buzzy bees all drinking wine,
One got drunk and then there were nine.

Nine busy buzzy bees they all went to a meeting,
One was very late and then there were eight.

Eight busy buzzy bees all talking about Heaven,
One rose up and then there were seven.

Seven busy buzzy bees they all got in a mix,
Then they got out they found there were six.

Six busy buzzy bees they all went to the pool,
One dared to dive and then there were five.

Five busy buzzy bees they all had a feast,
They all wanted more and then there were four.

Four busy buzzy bees all went into town,
One went to get a key then there were three.

Three busy buzzy bees they all went to the loo,
One fell down and then there were two.

Two busy buzzy bees they went to the church,
One was gone and then there was one.

One busy buzzy bee she went to the park,
She found her little honey bun and then there was none.

*Lyndsay Elks  (10)*
**Orchard Community Primary School**

## TEN HAPPY FISHES

Ten happy fishes swimming in a line,
Along came a shark and then there were nine.

Nine happy fishes swimming in a line,
One had a date and then there were eight.

Eight happy fishes swimming in a line,
One went to Heaven and then there were seven.

Seven happy fishes swimming in a line,
One found a stick and then there were six.

Six happy fishes swimming in a line,
One took a dive and then there were five.

Five happy fishes swimming in a line,
One discovered a door and then there were four.

Four happy fishes swimming in a line,
One found a cup of tea and then there were three.

Three happy fishes swimming in a line,
One went to the loo and then there were two.

Two happy fishes swimming in a line,
One was gone and then there was one.

One lonely fish swimming on its own,
It sung a song and then it was gone.

*Craig Nash (10)*
**Orchard Community Primary School**

# CLOCKS

*Tick-tock, tick-tock.*
Big clocks, small clocks,
Hanging on the wall clocks.
Gold and wooden,
Silver and bronze,
Even ones that sound like gongs.
Digital and handmade clocks,
Jazzy clocks that really rock.
*Tick-tock, tick-tock.*
No sound clocks, round clocks,
Only just found clocks.
Computer clocks, TV clocks,
Radio clocks, CD clocks.
*Tick-tock, tick-tock.*
Where would we be without clocks?

*James Curtis (10)*
*Orchard Community Primary School*


# ANIMALS

One slimy snake sliming through the room.
Two tiny ants crawling round the lounge.
Three trendy bears trampling round and round.
Four frightened fish swimming through the tank.
Five funky frogs hopping round the pond.
Six slow snails making slimy trails.
Seven stubborn spiders sneaking round the hall.
Eight terrible tigers prowling round the cage.
Nine naughty hyenas giggling round the garden.
Ten terrible turtles trudging round on the path.

*Gemma Baldy (9)*
*Orchard Community Primary School*

## THE FIVE FAT BEARS

Five fat bears sitting on the floor,
One rolled off and then there were four.

Four fat bears standing on a tree,
One fell out and then there were three.

Three fat bears bouncing on the loo,
One fell through and then there were two.

Two fat bears carrying a ton,
One got squished and then there was one.

One fat bear acting like a nun,
He got caught and then there were none.

*Michael Sheehan  (10)*
*Orchard Community Primary School*


## HAPPINESS

Happiness with her is a lovely thing.
A day without her seems like a month to me.
People always say that she is so lucky.
Poetry is her and happiness is me.
I am happy that she is here with me.
No one could say that she is nasty or horrible.
Elegant is she like a flower.
She shimmers in the morning and all through the day.
She is my mum and happiness is her.

*Sophie Tyler  (9)*
*Orchard Community Primary School*

## WHY DAD?

Why do footballers wear kits Dad?
Why is a football round Dad?
Why do footballers wear boots Dad?
Why do football teams have a logo Dad?
Why do football teams have a stadium Dad?
Why do you have to have a ref Dad?
Why is a football pitch rectangular Dad?
Why are there different divisions Dad?
Why do football teams have names Dad?
Why are there football rules Dad?
Why do footballers get paid a lot Dad?
Dad, one more question please.
Who invented football?
*Shut up!*

**Sophie Bucknall  (9)**
**Orchard Community Primary School**


## MOTORBIKES

M  ean machines around the track,
O  n and on through every lap.
T  o the pits and out again,
O  bservant watchers see the crash.
R  evving engines on the straight,
B  reaking records every day.
I  n and out of the chicanes,
K  TM's on the trail,
E  dging closer to the flag.

**Ryan Oakley  (9)**
**Orchard Community Primary School**

## IN SPACE

The dog on the moon
Saw a bridge joining
The moon to Venus.

And he saw aliens in Mars
By the stars or light gas showers
That try to rule you.

On Jupiter lasers
Come dangerously at
You.

Then the aliens
And the dog
Are friends.

*Patrick Dawson  (10)*
**Orchard Community Primary School**


## ITCHY INSECTS

Bad, beastly bugs
Small, spooky spiders
Fierce, flying flies
Silly, slimy slugs
Buzzy, buzzy bees
Lovely, little ladybirds
And wonderful wasps.

*James Elkins  (10)*
**Orchard Community Primary School**

## FRIENDS

F  riends can be a nuisance like my friend Mandy,
R  achel's very laidback but nothing compared to Sandy.
I  sobel talks and never really stops,
E  lizabeth is naughty and is always involved with cops.
N  atasha's really sweet,
D  oreen's really, really neat,
S  o I have *you* left to meet.

*Helen Sleigh (10)*
**Orchard Community Primary School**


## CAKE

Charlotte said, 'I think I'll bake,
A most delicious sponge cake.'
She took some lemons and mixed them up,
While adding water from a cup.
Then some branches from a tree,
She flicked off every flea and gave them to me.
Special gravel from the park,
Also some mouldy tree bark.
A thistle and a dash of sand,
She whipped it all up by hand.
On the top she wrote 'To You',
The way she said the bakers do.
Then she signed it fondly 'C'
And gave the whole of it to me.
I said to her, 'But I wouldn't dream
Of eating cake without whipped cream.'

*Lauren Bestwick (10)*
**St Bartholomew's CE Primary School, Loughborough**

## THE STORM

Rain, rain, lashing down
Making every child frown

The thunder clashing in the air
Just outside the dragon's lair

The dragon's roar spreads the world
The lightning comes down like being hurled

The dragon is now in flight
The thunder's like a flashing light

The monster stomps on the ground
While the hail makes a dreadful sound.

*Joshua Selby (11)*
*St Bartholomew's CE Primary School, Loughborough*


## ON THE FAIRGROUND!

Faster and faster, round and round
Speeding round the track
And the fairground sound
Went *pack, pack, pack!*

Off we go round the corner, on the ghost train
Ride and ride, feel the pain
On the spooky ghost train
We jump off, we find another roller coaster

Now we go up to the top
Off we go
My ears go *pop!*
But I cannot say no.

*Alex Eaton (10)*
*St Bartholomew's CE Primary School, Loughborough*

## IN THE DEEP

I jump into the water with a big bang
Just like a burst balloon
In five minutes I reach the ocean floor

In those five minutes I saw lots of fish
Then suddenly a shark came
So I swam and swam as fast as a racing car!

Once I reached the ocean floor
I swam, swam from one rock to another
Then suddenly I thought I was going too fast

Oh yes, look what I've found
A shipwreck, it looks battered
As a dustbin sight

When I went inside the ship
I saw a treasure chest, it had a gold handle
And I could pick it up, the treasure chest was hairy like an elephant

Just then I thought I'd go back and find the right equipment
So I went back up
As I swam, swam, I saw lots of fish

Finally I reached the top of the water
And climbed onto the boat
Mate, I forgot my equipment

I went back down and scraped away seaweed from the treasure chest
Then I swam up to the side of the boat
And tied a knot in a bit of string

Then I tugged three times on the string
And the treasure chest came with a big bang like a balloon
I swam back up as I had run out of air

I said to my mate that my day was done
So how about we go home
And have some tea.

**Harry Collinson (9)**
*St Bartholomew's CE Primary School, Loughborough*


## THE SNORKELLER

I see children splashing in the sea,
Like seals splashing in the water when they're playing,
I see children playing as I go down into the water.

I see crabs scuttling on the sand,
I see flat fish hiding in the sand,
Like children playing hide-and-seek.

I see lobsters digging deep,
Like diggers digging up sand,
I see fish swimming by,
I see shellfish hiding on rocks,
As still as statues.

I see children swimming in the water,
Like crocodiles as I swim up,
Because it is getting too cold,
As I come out of the water
I say goodbye to the fish and the sea and go.

**Sophie Middleton (9)**
*St Bartholomew's CE Primary School, Loughborough*

## THE SNORKELLER

I look into the sky and I see
Seagulls swooshing down
I like the wind blowing the sand around
It's like raindrops falling into your eyes
It makes your eyes sting like onion in pies
On the shore there are children telling lies

I plunge below the salty water
Like a dolphin jumping in mid-air
I let myself drop into the water just like a pear
I finally reach the bottom of the rocky lair
There is an explosion of shrimps, *bang!*
But I couldn't help but stare.

I finally see what I'm looking for
It is a ship on the rocky floor
It is wrecked under the splashing water
There it is, a bar of gold upon a solid rock
Over there in the corner is a shark, just about to bite

I pick up the gold and swim ashore
I see children once again playing
Some of them are sitting there bored
Some are splashing in the water
Finally I'm in the ordinary world once again.

*Damon Barber (9)*
*St Bartholomew's CE Primary School, Loughborough*

## THE SNORKELLER

I look out at the sunset as orange as a peach,
The waves gently, gently lapping against the boat.

I go splashing into the water from the shiny red boat
And set off into the distance as blue as the sky.

I go under with a splash and disappear from sight,
The world suddenly goes as dark as a starless sky.

I swim on through the seaweed as green as grass
Whooshing on and on and suddenly I stop.

I stop to see a school of fish, as colourful as a rainbow,
They pass on swiftly, I carry on swooping through the sea.

I find an old shipwreck with rings round the windows,
                              as crusty as old nails,
*Bang* goes the old ship's door as I open it.

Inside the ship, I find gold as bright as a button,
*Creak* goes a chest as I open it.

Inside the chest, I find pearls as round as the moon,
*Click* goes the chest as I close it again.

I come out of the ship as fast as a fish,
*Swish* goes a dolphin's fins.

I grab on to the dolphin and *whoosh!* Up I go,
I am up again and there are stars in the sky
As bright as can be, I'm back in the real world.

***Bryony Unwin  (10)***
**St Bartholomew's CE Primary School, Loughborough**

## THE SNORKELLER

I see whales playing in the water,
Like rain falling in a storm,
I see seaweed wiggling,
Like worms getting out of a hole.

I see fish swimming,
Like a flash of lighting.
I see crabs crawling on the rocks,
Like babies crawling on the floor.

I see a shipwreck wrecked,
Like a battered-up car.
I see a shiny thing,
Like a sapphire.

I swim to the ship,
Like a flash of lightning.
I find gold bars shining,
Like stars.

I find eight pieces of gold
Shining like glitter.
I grab some
And swim back safely to the surface.

*Laurie Anderson  (9)*
**St Bartholomew's CE Primary School, Loughborough**

## FUNNY CATS

Old Mr Fribbles has long whiskers
As long as his sister's
Every cat in the countryside went to see the mayor
But he's just a downright hare
One of the cats was so fat
He didn't look where he sat!
A cat had a little jerk
Then the countryside went berserk!
There was also a cat
With a black top hat
A cat dug a hole
In his fishy bowl
Another cat likes eating sleet
I think that's all he can eat
One cat put up his middle claw
And he ended up breaking a law
Then a cat stood on a tail
And it was very pale
*Roooaarrr!*

***Edward Rusak-Plant (8)***
*St Bartholomew's CE Primary School, Loughborough*


## ALIENS ARE COMING

As the little alien came near
I saw he was holding a bottle of beer
His spacecraft glowed red and white
As his ship flew through the night
A beam of light shot through the air
Suddenly I fell in despair.

***Ben Sinfield (10)***
*St Bartholomew's CE Primary School, Loughborough*

## MY FAMILY

*Gemma*
Gemma is like a stubborn ram
She never ever gives in
Although she knows she's sometimes wrong
She always has to win

*Dad*
My dad is really very strong
And also very brave
He is fun and very friendly
Unless I misbehave

*Mum*
My mum is always very busy
But when she plays with me
We play games and have lots of fun
And at night we watch TV

*Me*
I am very smart and tidy
My room is always clean
I think that I am nice and kind
And never ever mean.

**Daniel Barby  (9)**
**St Bartholomew's CE Primary School, Loughborough**

## SNOW

Crystal snow all around,
What have I found?
The gentle, lovely snow sounds.

Calling my friends,
The snow curves around the bends,
That's what my mum sends.

The white blobs in the sky,
High in the sky like they're flying,
The weather is never lying.

Snowflakes falling down,
They are falling on my head,
That's what I said.

Getting a scarf in the house,
Just like a snowy, cheeky mouse,
Going out to the snow wind.

Skiing on the frozen ice,
Being really kind and nice,
Going to my friend's house.

*Laura Connolly (8)*
*St Bartholomew's CE Primary School, Loughborough*

## SWEET LAND

The land where marshmallows fall from the sky
And candy sticks have wings and fly.
The land where ladies are real lollipops
And the gingerbread men dance around and hop.
The land where grass is not green
And muffins sneak around unseen.
The land where chocolate buttons are treasured in chests
And where the baby bubblegums are little pests!
The land where mud is as sticky as toffee
And the sea is as sweet as chocolate.
The land where the sky is brown with Galaxy
And lots of magic stars laugh, *tee-hee!*
The land where houses are rich chocolate bars
And where people rely on strawberry laces for a car!
The land which you so cannot guess,
It is of course, the land which is now in a terrible *mess!*

*Isabelle Carter (9)*
*St Bartholomew's CE Primary School, Loughborough*


## THE BUTTERFLY

The butterfly with colours so bright,
Even brighter than a light.
They fly away,
Or stay all day.
Caterpillars, green and brown,
See when they can fly around.
They're crying out so loud and clear,
To see when you are very near.
Landing on the leaves, they dream
For most of the day or so it seems.

*Emma Russell (8)*
*St Bartholomew's CE Primary School, Loughborough*

## THE HANDBAG

The wind is blowing down the street,
Hold tight to your handbag.
'Let go,' the wind said,
'No, no,' said the handbag.

The sun is shining in the sky.
The handbag is very heavy.
'Let go,' the hand said,
'No, no,' I will not.

The handbag full of all good things,
I'll hold tight to the hand.
No one is going to make me let go,
'No one,' said the handbag.

It's cold today.
The handbag slips from my cold hand,
Onto the grass it fell.
All the good things fell to the ground,
'Oh dear,' the handbag said.

I think I'm just made for the summer,
A beach I'll find instead.
So into the sun I'll go next time,
Into the sun I'll go.

Where no wind blows,
No cold hand to feel,
Just sand to fall on,
Warm and soft.
That's the life for me.

*Holly Lacey  (8)*
*St Bartholomew's CE Primary School, Loughborough*

## SUMMER

I love summer when I swim in a pool
I love summer when I keep nice and cool
I love summer when I drink a milkshake
I love summer when I eat biscuits my mum bakes

I love summer if I go on holiday
I love summer when we watch the ships on the bay
I love summer when I have ice cream
I love summer when I see the sun's beam

I love summer when I see my best friends
I love summer but I'm very sad when it ends
I love summer when the sun appears in the sky
I love summer but don't want to say goodbye

I love summer when I go for short walks
I love summer when I hear my parrot talk
I love summer when I go on long bike rides
I love summer when I wear sunglasses that cover my eyes

I love summer when we play in the park
I love summer when it doesn't get dark
I love summer when I see the sun
I love summer when I eat a sugared bun

I love summer when I stay up very late
I love summer when we go to the fête
I love summer when we go strawberry picking
I love summer when I go with my dad fishing.

*Felicity Norris  (9)*
*St Bartholomew's CE Primary School, Loughborough*

## WINTER SNOW

Slippery snow slides out of the sky,
Long thin icicles,
From the windowpane, rain trickles from the sky
And makes floods,
The cows eat their cuds,
Bright colour from the presents, green and red
And on Christmas Day you get out of bed,
Turkey waiting for the plate
And everyone is late.
Boxing Day, the birds are out to play,
Mince pies are hot, but the snow is not.
Bacon rashers in the pan
And now get up you lazy old man
And for dinner we have got lamb with jam.

*Christopher Swain  (8)*
*St Bartholomew's CE Primary School, Loughborough*


## FRIENDS

Friends are kind and respectful,
They help you when you fall over,
They stick up for you and try to protect you from bullies,
They help when you ask them to,
They are thoughtful and sharing,
Friends are helpful and caring,
If you don't have a ruler or pen,
They will lend you one,
Then encourage you in hard races,
They help you with words that you don't understand,
They invite you to stay and play,
All this is what a good friend should be.

*John Timerick  (8)*
*St Bartholomew's CE Primary School, Loughborough*

## CHOCOLATE

Chocolate, chocolate smells so sweet
It smells so sweet from your head to your feet
Chocolate, chocolate is very nice
It is so cool, so think the mice
Chocolate, chocolate everywhere
Mum doesn't like it, but I don't care

Toffee, Smarties and Galaxy too
All go in my mouth for me to chew
Chocolate, chocolate is so yummy
I love it when it hits my tummy
I always want more and more
But sometimes it makes my tummy sore

Chocolate melts in the sun
And you can also have it on a bun
Chocolate is so sticky
It can also be a little tricky
When it's running off your ice cream
Now that's what I really call a dream!

*Ryan Beecham (8)*
*St Bartholomew's CE Primary School, Loughborough*


## LIGHTNING

Lightning, crashing down to the ground
The clouds travelling all around
Clouds firing lightning with the speed of light
Lighting up, the darkened sky, bright
Lightning, striking the old oak tree
Lightning, sets it free
Lighting, gives people a fright
Sometimes it flashes in the night.

*Pedram Amirkhalili (9)*
*St Bartholomew's CE Primary School, Loughborough*

## THE FORTRESS

Seized at night was the fortress,
Black, grey and white.
Its iron gates where shut and locked.
Guards examined the grounds,
Looking for strangers all around.
The hideous enemy
Charged at the gates.
The gates resisted.
The army charged once more,
Still the gates resisted.
They charged once more,
The gates crumbled at
The enemy's feet.
*'Charge!'* they shouted.
*Cling! Clang!* went the swords,
As they clattered together.
Arrows shot like the whistling wind,
Guards bashed together,
Feeling the fortress,
The battle had just begun!

*Tom Parslow  (8)*
*St Bartholomew's CE Primary School, Loughborough*


## TRAIN

Red and black steam train
Moving a hundred miles an hour
Steam coming out
Whooshing like wind against a metal dish
Hissing and chuffing down the valley
Destination - next station.

*Timothy Barrass  (8)*
*St Bartholomew's CE Primary School, Loughborough*

## ANIMALS

There are lots of animals in the world,
Some of them even go to sleep when they're curled.
Sometimes they don't do what they're told
And some even hibernate when it gets cold.
Mice, gerbils, hamsters and rats,
Lions, tigers, panthers and cats.

Cats and dogs are used as pets,
When they get ill, they go the vet's.
Some have wings, like chickens and birds
And of course they can't speak in words.
Zebras, gorillas, monkeys and dogs,
Fishes, sharks, whales and frogs.

Some have babies like puppies or cubs
And some feed in little grey tubs.
Some sleep in the very dark night
And some sleep when it's light.
Goats, sheep, lambs and oxes,
Wolves, dogs, coyotes and foxes.

Lots of fishes are very small,
But most don't hurt you at all.
Some are fun and like to play,
But some keep you up all day.
Chickens, birds, parrots and owls,
Horses, cows, pigs and fowls.

Some like it on a farm
And some like to stay calm.
Some animals can jump high,
But it is sad when they die.
Leopards, cheetahs, snakes and whales,
Jaguars, turtles, bears and quails.

*John Vale  (9)*
*St Bartholomew's CE Primary School, Loughborough*

## DIVING IN THE DEEP!

Upon the surface I see the sparkling sea splashing everywhere,
I see seagulls swooping,
Windsurfers are surfing
And the sun is shining over there.

I plunge down to the ocean below,
Seaweed swishing like trees in the wind,
Fishes of all beautiful colours,
Shrimps and crabs moving so slow.

What is that softly shimmering,
I swim closer – curious to see,
Passing coral as sharp as daggers,
It is gold, gold gently glimmering.

There's more in the shipwreck,
With skeletons and swords,
Clanking as loud as fireworks,
Jumping, shouting and dancing on the deck.

Ow! A crab just pinched me,
With claws like scissors,
It twists the skin
And taps away like a buzzy bee.

I must swim to the surface,
With my gold as precious as life
And knowledge of the deep,
Passing the crackling coral on the ocean base.

I walk across the sand,
Watching children playing,
With buckets as bright as buttons
And my jewels jangling in my hand.

*Hannah Iley (10)*
*St Bartholomew's CE Primary School, Loughborough*

# THE SNORKELLER

I see children booming about,
Like people rushing in a city.
I plunge down into the water's depths,
Like a missile firing in the water.
I see a shark zooming about,
Like a car rushing into town.
I see a dolphin whistling his song,
Like a gym leader whistling his whistle.
I see fish swishing around,
Like a twister in the sky.
I see the sea plants swaying around,
Like a fan blowing about.
I see gems sparkling in the sea,
Like the sun shining in the sky.
I pop back up to the surface,
Like a shark pouncing on its prey.

*Matthew Watson  (10)*
*St Bartholomew's CE Primary School, Loughborough*


# THE SNORKELLER

I put on my snorkel fast and dived into the dark blue sea,
Seaweed waving upon the reef, like trees swaying side to side.
Tropical fish eating stones like humans munching away at nice food.
People's legs wiggling along like swaying dull flowers.
I see an old brown sailing boat, with sharks swimming in and out.
Boats' shadows swinging up and down upon the waves.
I see the sun peeking through the clouds and the dark salty waves.
I see children plunging in and out, playing in the sea.
I see people swimming into the deep, deep sea,
Then diving under like submarines.
Seagulls swooping up and down, eating people's chips.

*Harry Newcombe  (9)*
*St Bartholomew's CE Primary School, Loughborough*

# ELLA MCSTUMPING

Ella McStumping
Was fond of jumping
From tables and chairs
Bookshelves and stairs
She would jump to the floor
Then climb back for more
At the age of 3
She climbed a high tree
Doctor McSpetter
Says she'll get better
Now Ella McStumping
Has given up jumping.

*Lauren Beech (8)*
*St Bartholomew's CE Primary School, Loughborough*


# MUSIC

Music, music in the air,
Music, music everywhere.
Music of the clarinet,
It never makes me upset!
Music of the piano,
Probably most popular, but I don't know!
Music of a didgeridoo,
Came from the country of the kangaroo.
Music of the flute,
Very nice sound, *toot toot!*
Music is where I am found,
Music, music all around.

*Charlotte Robinson (8)*
*St Bartholomew's CE Primary School, Loughborough*

## SUMMERTIME

S   ummer is very hot
U   nder an umbrella
M   y friend, Emily and I
M   elt in the heat
E   very day
R   elaxing with a drink

T   he trees are giving us shade
I   'm hot and sweaty
M   e and my sister, Laura play in the sun
E   ating ice cream.

*Kate Smith  (8)*
*St Bartholomew's CE Primary School, Loughborough*


## THE FLICKER FLAME!

A
Fiery hear,
A fiery glaze.
A flicker, a glimmer
Now gone within days.
Logs are thrown on to keep up full colour.
Flames are leaping fuller and fuller.
Climbing up to their height,
Try to be careful, it might want a bite.
Put over its safe fireguard
Now it won't eat your best birthday card!
Hot and warm, warm and hot,
Keep all the ashes in a dark little pot.
Fire, fire!

*Sophie Parslow  (10)*
*St Bartholomew's CE Primary School, Loughborough*

## SEASONS

Orange and red the autumn sky
Up and up, far up high
Browny-red and yellow leaves
Tumbling down for all to see

Grey and murky winter sky
Delicate snowflakes glinting by
A white blanket all around
Icy and slippery on the ground

Light blue and grey the spring sky
Birds soaring gliding by
New shoots growing up
A new hatchling, a baby rook

Bright and blue the summer sky
Sunbeams gleaming far up high
Turquoise sea swamped with fishes
Children on sand thinking wishes.

*Ursula Rae (11)*
*St Bartholomew's CE Primary School, Loughborough*


## SPIDERS

A spider spins a lovely web to catch,
To catch its prey each day.
A fly gets caught in the web,
Its wings are wrapped and trapped.
A wasp sees the fly in the web,
He flies in low and slow,
But the spider comes from the web
And catches and traps him dead.

*Ryan Hopewell (10)*
*St Bartholomew's CE Primary School, Loughborough*

## SPACE

Space stretches out in all different directions,
North, east, south and west,
But nobody has travelled beyond our galaxy,
So how do we know that ours is the best,
Aliens could be plotting an evil plan,
To destroy the human race.
They would kill every single man
And destroy the Earth's face.
They could come in one enormous fleet,
Looking for a battle to fight.
They would have 1 eye, 3 noses and 15 feet,
They might attack at night,
So my dream draws to an end,
It hopefully won't come true.
So I'll talk to a listening friend,
I think I'll tell a few.

*Sam Russell  (11)*
*St Bartholomew's CE Primary School, Loughborough*


## I HAVE A MATE . . .

I have a mate
She's really great
She says she loves to paint
We went fishing and she ate all the bait
I have another mate which I really hate
She has a really horrid plate
She went to a fête
And she found some slate
Now her mum says she has to be a saint.

*Emily Richards  (10)*
*St Bartholomew's CE Primary School, Loughborough*

# THE SNORKELLER

Seagulls splashing in the sea,
Like a bird that cannot see,
Surfers surfing on the waves,
People finding secret caves.

I plunge into the waters deep,
Oysters waking from their sleep,
Crabs are creeping on the sand,
Ow! that crab's just bitten my hand.

I swim and see a ghostly ship,
In the sails I see a rip,
I swim inside, then gold I steal,
Like a hippo having a meal.

I see crabs scuttling around,
Like an ant on the ground.
Then a crab gives a nasty nip,
Ow! What a dirty trick.

I swim past little coloured fish,
They would make a tasty dish.
Up to the surface, back I glide,
With a turtle at my side.

*Dan Mousley  (9)*
*St Bartholomew's CE Primary School, Loughborough*


# POPPY

P    oppies
O    f remembrance
P    retty and peaceful
P    oppies
Y    early.

*Ben Taylor  (10)*
*St Bartholomew's CE Primary School, Loughborough*

## SWEETS

Yummy! Yummy! Sweeties!
Really good treaties
I like eating sherbet lemons
They turn my tongue green
It's the worst colour ever seen

Sweeties are so chewy
They are very, very gooey
When they get stuck to my tooth
My mum, she hits the roof

Red, blue, green and pink
So many colours, I cannot think
I must choose quickly
But they all look so sticky!

The ones that I chose were whizzing balls
I could eat them all day
Unfortunately you do have to pay
*But then!*
I got a lot of them anyway!

***Joel Hardcastle (9)***
*St Bartholomew's CE Primary School, Loughborough*


## SPIDER

*S*pooky
*P*etrifying
t*I*ny
*D*eadly
st*E*althly
Cleve*R*.

***Edward Mear (11)***
*St Bartholomew's CE Primary School, Loughborough*

## I DREAMED A DREAM

I dreamed a dream of little spiders,
I cannot tell you why,
But in my dream I saw a spider's web,
Being spun so very high.

They toddled beneath a bramble bush,
A tiny fly in a web was trying to escape,
A spider moved towards it in a rush,
Covered in a dark black cape.

I watched the spider spin its steely web
And then it scuttled by,
It sat still, missing a leg,
Underneath the sunny sky.

I dreamed a dream of little spiders,
I cannot tell you why,
But in my dream I saw its web,
Being spun so very high.

*Joshua Kirk (10)*
*St Bartholomew's CE Primary School, Loughborough*


## SCHOOL LIFE

Some children don't like to go to school,
Other children think it's way cool.
It's true that maths and spelling can get boring,
I much prefer art and drawing.
Boys think they are really great,
But I would rather have a girl as my mate.
Sometimes my teacher gets cross,
That's all right because he is the big boss.

*Sophie Foster (8)*
*St Bartholomew's CE Primary School, Loughborough*

## THERE IS A BIT OF EVIL IN EVERYONE

There is a bit of evil in everyone
In the roar of a lion and the songbird's song
In the deep dark depths of a dismal lake
And in the rumbling groan of a huge earthquake

There is a bit of evil in everyone
It hides behind corners and lurks in a throng
When it is near, we shiver and shake
It will do wrong, for the Devil's sake

There is a bit of evil in everyone
In the hiss of a snake and the church bells' dong
In the voice of a loved one and the voice of a friend
And you get the impression that this must be the end.

There is a bit of evil in everyone.

*Leo May (11)*
*St Bartholomew's CE Primary School, Loughborough*


## PETRIFIED

He was coming closer
I couldn't take it
'No Sir, no Sir, no Sir!'

My eyelids got weaker
They started to water
'Help me, help me, help me!'

His face got meaner
He started to speak . . .

'That's the best piece of work I've ever seen!'

*Naomi Shipway (11)*
*St Bartholomew's CE Primary School, Loughborough*

## BIRD OF PREY

The bird of prey breaks out of its egg,
Trying to find a secure place to put its spiny leg,
His mother comes to feed her chick,
Looking after her baby so he doesn't get sick.

The chick is no more a chick and is ready to try and fly,
His mother gazes over him as he gently floats by,
Now to hunt his first victim he spots a rat,
Dived down, but swooped back up for lurching at him was a mad cat.

Now he is a few years older and time to leave the nest,
Years have gone on and the bird has always done his best,
Been careful around humans but once out hunting he let his guard down
And *bang* the bird of prey lay there, ever more in rest.

*Hannah Brennan-Mee (11)*
*St Bartholomew's CE Primary School, Loughborough*


## THE SPRING AND SUMMER SEASON

Spring is full of life and love,
With little heads popping out of the ground.
A white bird flutters by,
A dove in fact,
Flying above my head making no sound.

Summer is full of heat and warmth,
On the beach,
People were playing in the sand,
Dancing to their favourite pop band

And that is the story of spring and summer.

*Nathalie Dawson (11)*
*St Bartholomew's CE Primary School, Loughborough*

## THE SNORKELLER

I see people playing in the sand
I hear waves crashing on the rocks
I plunge into the ferocious sea
I see fish swimming around me

I see a shipwreck covered in seaweed
I find some gold inside the ship
Shining brighter than stars
I find a very big treasure chest

In the treasure chest I find
Shining diamonds and pearls
Then two sharks appear
I zoom off as fast as a cheetah

I hear the sharks following me
Whooshing close behind me
As fast as lightning
Then I reach the shore, safe at last.

*Harry Thirlby (9)*
*St Bartholomew's CE Primary School, Loughborough*


## POETRY

C omputers are very intelligent,
O n the contrary, very elegant,
M agically very fast,
P ainfully they don't last,
U nfortunately they crash,
T otally a lot of cash,
E very day we play games,
R ight until it bursts into flames.

*Stephen Maddocks (10)*
*St Bartholomew's CE Primary School, Loughborough*

## MY FAMILY

My auntie Sue
Has now got the flu,
She caught it from me
When I went to see
My little cousin called Bea.

My uncle Jack
Has got a bad back.
He leant on a nail,
Then stepped in a pail,
When trying to pick up the mail.

My cousin Sam
Is going out with Pam.
To show his love
He bought her a dove
And that's the story of Sam and Pam.

*Rachel McCoubrie  (11)*
*St Bartholomew's CE Primary School, Loughborough*


## THE WINTER

The winter is great
It's fun and I can't wait
To be throwing the snow
In my brother's face
Somewhere, some place
It's as soft as dough
The snow is as white as rice
And I'm making a snowman that needs
A head and body
While my brother is skating on the ice.

*Caleb Roberts  (10)*
*St Bartholomew's CE Primary School, Loughborough*

## THE DAYDREAM

The day I had a dream
I dreamt I was on a team
We lost 3-1
Then I bit my tongue

I woke up in a state
Then realised it was the school fête
I went to have a drink
Then dropped the glass in the sink

I was so ashamed I ran away
And couldn't stay to act in the play
I tripped over on the gravel floor
Then I banged into the door

Then I woke up!

*Bethany Coy  (11)*
*St Bartholomew's CE Primary School, Loughborough*


## COLOUR

I like red because it is the colour of my bed.
I like blue because it reminds me of you.
I like black because it is the colour of Santa's sack.
I like green because it is the colour I have seen.
I like purple because it is the colour of the circle.
I like grey because it is the colour of hay.
I like yellow because it makes me say hello.
I like pink because it is the colour of my sink.
I like brown because it is the colour of my crown.
I like gold because I am old.

*Amy Paramore  (9)*
*St Bartholomew's CE Primary School, Loughborough*

## THE SHARK DIVER

The sky is lit by the moon and the stars are shining,
I stare at the water like an owl, then I splash in the sea.
The water is cold and strange,
I see a dark shadow and plunge.
The shadow is the remains of a shipwreck.

I see a dusty chest, it opens with a creak,
The gold and sapphires shine in the light.
I see a shark ready to bite,
The gold is in my hand,
I swim from the shark and his band.

The sharks get nearer and nearer,
I see the light get nearer,
The sharks get a new sense,
I see them splash away,
The sharks are as silly as a sausage.

I am now running out of air,
The light is now fading,
I am now falling like a rock, *slam!*
The coastguard awakes me,
I am back on land, I am free!

*Toby Steel (10)*
*St Bartholomew's CE Primary School, Loughborough*


## TIGER

sTripy
sIlent
rippinG
Execution
hunteR.

*Jack Graham (10)*
*St Bartholomew's CE Primary School, Loughborough*

## THE SNORKELLER

I see fish swimming like boats
I see children splashing around like seagulls
I dive down into the deep depths
The water is as cold as ice
So I have to go up to the surface
I see dolphins jumping up and down like kangaroos
I see children playing like seals happily
I see sharks circling round and round
Like cars on a roundabout
I see adults buying drinks like lightning
For them and their kids
Like people going shopping
I see crabs scuttling on the sand like birds
I see flat fish dancing like dancers.

*Max Wootton (10)*
*St Bartholomew's CE Primary School, Loughborough*


## IN THE NET

The blood is rushing,
The manager's heart is thumping,
The fans are singing,
They are all waiting for the beginning.

The whistle blows,
Off the centre forward goes,
Running left, running right,
Quorn Juniors put up a good fight.

Josh passes the ball
To Ross who beats them all,
He smacks the ball in,
Quorn Juniors have another win.

*Ross Gartshore (10)*
*St Bartholomew's CE Primary School, Loughborough*

## DOWN IN THE DEEP

I see the beach,
A sheet of silk,
But it's really rough underfoot.
As I plunge down,
Into the deep waters,
I think of a freezer and ice,
The water is cold,
As cold as the snow,
I'm shivering, slithering down.
I see swaying seaweed,
In red, green and brown,
As slimy as slugs,
I weave in and out.
I swim further on,
Fish tails flapping,
As flimsy as feathers,
Covered in stripes,
Coated in colour.
As I swim on,
I discover a ship,
As still as a statue,
Not a creak or a crack.
I swim through the wood,
All broken and splintered,
I gasp,
I suck up water like a vacuum cleaner.
*Whoosh!*
I swim up as fast as a rocket,
Gulp! A breath of fresh air,
But what a disappointment
Down in the deep.

*Hannah Wilson  (10)*
*St Bartholomew's CE Primary School, Loughborough*

## THE SNORKELLER AND HIS LUNCH

I see children plunging into the sea
Like small wriggly electric eels
I see water swirling up and down
I decide to go right, right down

I see huge crowds of fish going swish
Like tons of schoolboys
I see a big fish that will make a lovely snack

I see fish zooming into coral
Like bullets flying as quick as sound
I climb round and round the coral
Searching, searching for my dinner

I see, I search like a hawk
Swooping, swishing round corners
Flash, flash, what was that?
Jellyfish, what a snack

I see dogfish, *snap, snap, snap*
Like a hungry shark
They always make a lot of sound
I am searching for my dinner

I see gems sparkling like the moon
They're not gems, they're eyes
*Snap! Snap!* Help, a shark,
When am I going to get dinner?

I see dinner in my sight
Like diamonds sparkling
*Slap, slap*, goes my lips
Dinner's mine

Tuna, clams, tuna, clams
I am going up for my dinner.

*Alex Francis  (10)*
*St Bartholomew's CE Primary School, Loughborough*

## THE SNORKELLER

I saw the waves splashing against the rocky beach,
Like the Titanic crashing into an iceberg,
Then I plunged
Into the deep blue sea.
I saw lots of different fish,
Swimming faster and faster,
Like a racing car speeding along the tracks,
Then I saw a sunken ship.
I searched the ship that swayed when the fish rushed passed,
I saw a trunk full of treasure sparkling like sapphires,
I opened the trunk.
I saw dozens of diamonds and rubies floating about,
Like tiny ants having a dance
And then I brought them back up
To the surface while everyone clapped.

*Gemma Adkin (10)*
*St Bartholomew's CE Primary School, Loughborough*


## FOOTBALL

*F*un
*O*ffering prices
g*O*al
s*T*adium
*B*all
*A*ttacking
Goa*L* kick
Goa*L* post.

*Alex Honour (11)*
*St Bartholomew's CE Primary School, Loughborough*

## THE FOUR SEASONS OF THE YEAR

In the summer, the sun is shining,
Instead of rain falling as hard as rock,
The sun is out, how very surprising,
Every step I take the day gets warmer.

In spring, the rain is back,
The foxes out to catch their prey,
Everybody stays indoors,
While lonely animals try to live another day.

In the autumn, the leaves are falling,
Coats and hats are coming on,
Insects are creeping and crawling,
Looking for a place to stay.

In the winter, children are as happy as ever,
*Crash, bang, creak,*
The children throwing snowballs,
While the animals are fast asleep.

**Thomas Hayes (10)**
*St Bartholomew's CE Primary School, Loughborough*


## THE SEASONS

In spring, bulbs grow up through the soil,
In summer the bright sun beams all day,
In autumn all the leaves fall down
And in winter, it's Christmas Day.

**Gemma Barby (11)**
*St Bartholomew's CE Primary School, Loughborough*

## BULL FIGHT

With panting, snorting nostrils
And evil yellow eyes
And crooked, cracking, curling horns
Would make you want to cry

He will take no mercy
Or give the gentle moo
So do not wear red while there
Or he may aim at you!

Nothing can stop him
Nor can make him go
Except his favourite colour, red
For he's a deadly foe!

So I'd stay on your toes today
If you are going there
For he will charge like a raging ox
So if I were you, beware!

*Calum Rae (9)*
*St Bartholomew's CE Primary School, Loughborough*


## THE CANDLE

The light from my candle
Glowing in the dark
The candle looking down at my sandal
And the music from the gentle harp
Suddenly there was a turn on the door handle
And all I could hear was a dog's bark.

*Annabel Moore (10)*
*St Bartholomew's CE Primary School, Loughborough*

## SEASONS

The summer sky is bright blue,
Full of happiness all the time,
The cheerful sun is shining brightly,
It's hot!
The winter sky is dull grey,
Full of unhappiness all the time,
The moon is shining brightly,
It's cold!
The autumn sky is brown and orange,
Full of different colours all the time,
Animals playing in the leaves,
It's windy!
The spring sky is yellow,
Full with the brightness of daffodils,
Excited children eating Easter eggs,
It's sunny again.

*Kerrie Laverick  (10)*
*St Bartholomew's CE Primary School, Loughborough*


## AUTUMN

*Crunch* go all of the leaves under my feet,
Brown, yellow and red are my favourite colours in autumn.
We're trying to meet a hedgehog,
We will hopefully be lucky.
My feet are really mucky in the mud,
I love autumn.
My friends are playing in the leaves,
The trees are really bare.
Look, there it is, the hedgehog,
Autumn.

*Helen Askew  (11)*
*St Bartholomew's CE Primary School, Loughborough*

## FOOTBALL MATCH

F ootball on the playground,
O ne team against another,
O ur team has been together for years,
T here's Dan and James and Henry and Me,
B oys only of course and in Year 6,
A mbitious to win,
L osing,
L ike 1-0

M any voices shout and cheer but then . . .
A rgument starts,
T hen the fight starts,
C aught red-handed,
H eading to the headteacher's office.

*Jack Gerrity  (11)*
*St Bartholomew's CE Primary School, Loughborough*


## THEME PARK

I'm going to the fair today, don't question why,
My aim for today is to play and have fun,
The main thing on my mind though
Is to go on the big ride, the big ride.
As the big ride got closer
I started feeling the nerves,
They felt like aeroplanes whizzing around my tum,
When I got into the line, I started to watch the ride,
The cart looked like a rocket blasting through the stars,
When I got on the ride the nerves came back again,
I begged for mercy, pleaded with all my might,
My plea was granted,
I got off the ride, ran to the loo, don't question why!

*Jonathan Waller  (9)*
*St Bartholomew's CE Primary School, Loughborough*

## THE OCEAN

Down below the ocean blue,
I started wondering what I should do,
Tied to a rock, I was being killed,
But still full of hope I was filled,
The chain was rusty, I gave it a kick,
But it only snapped once I gave it a hit,
I swam to the shore, I was full of fresh glee,
But since I was scared, I needed a wee,
Even though I was wet, I lay in the sand,
Looking, looking, looking for a piece of land,
Sand stuck on my back, over my face,
I couldn't believe it's all over the place!
I went to the sea to wash it all off,
But when I came back I had a big cough!

*Sam Graham (9)*
*St Bartholomew's CE Primary School, Loughborough*


## THE DOLPHIN

Swimming up and down
Swimming round and round
Diving oh so deep
Making no sound

Seeing lots of fish
Having a good time
Splashing around in the water
Everything is fine

Following a boat
Speeding on the waves
The man is wearing a coat
Calling me a cutie.

*Katie Gerighty (9)*
*St Bartholomew's CE Primary School, Loughborough*

## SEASONS

In winter . . .
Crunching through the cold crisp snow,
As big as ten pence pieces, as cold as ice.
Curling up in front of a fire,
Warmth flooding over you, glad to be inside,
Playing in the snow.

In spring . . .
Prancing through warm dry grass,
Longer than you've ever seen, weather getting warmer,
Animals coming out of hibernation,
Scurrying through the undergrowth, as quick as lighting,
Playing in the grass.

In summer . . .
Splashing in the sea, foaming, flipping waves,
As tall as you, waves like swallowing mouths,
Sunbathing on soft, silky sand,
Having a rest with books and sunglasses,
Playing in the waves.

In autumn . . .
Crushing, crisping through dry leaves,
As light as a feather, warm to touch,
Animals collecting food, before the cold weather,
Soft, snug, smooth nests being made, ready to hibernate,
Playing in the leaves.

*Rebecca Andrews  (10)*
*St Bartholomew's CE Primary School, Loughborough*

## KITTEN

Jumping around everywhere,
Showing everyone that they care,
Chasing string all over the house,
Look over there! A scuttling mouse,
They never stop moving,
They're like a bird that never stops
Running away from water,
Like a magnet being pulled away,
Spinning, jumping and running all around the house,
Just like a top that will just spin and spin and spin,
Scratching birds as they would scratch the floor,
Ignoring their post, they start to do more,
Attacking, scratching and killing the floor,
As fluffy as a mitten,
Yes, I'm a *kitten.*

*Hannah Biffen (9)*
*St Bartholomew's CE Primary School, Loughborough*

# A SPOOKY NIGHT

It was a foggy night,
I was walking along the dock,
I saw a light,
On the floor there was a lock,
I looked up quickly,
I turned around as fast as I could,
There it stood something quite horrible,
Ran and I ran,
I don't think it was possible,
Thought I heard a bang,
Hoped and I hoped it was a dream,
I turned around,
I saw a big beam,
Then I heard a gruesome sound,
So there's a gruesome tale.

*Paul Rynton  (10)*
*St Bartholomew's CE Primary School, Loughborough*

## THE FIREBALL ROLLER COASTER

We walked over to the fireball roller coaster,
As we approached we could feel the tension building inside us,
It was now our turn, we stepped in and looked ahead at the
high looping tracks.

We started slow then we got faster, faster and faster still,
It was whooshing around the loops like a rocket round and up
and down, and round,
It was exactly like a fireball.

Our hair was sticking up and Tom was feeling great,
We were eating our hot dogs and the sauce was going all over our faces,
Our tummies tickled as we went round loops,
As we went down the last ramp, I was so relieved,
We were two minutes away from the end,
One minute we were going to get off this scary ride,
We stepped off looking back at that devastating ride.

*Thomas Andrews  (10)*
*St Bartholomew's CE Primary School, Loughborough*


## THE MONSTROUS BOOK OF MONSTERS

Marvel at the meaning of the monstrous book of monsters;
Mean monsters munch menacingly at McDonald's,
Moulding mummies moan for many midnight moons,
Murderous midgets and mites make monstrosities from corroding corpses,
Money-hungry mini-managers make millions,
. . . Now you have marvelled at the monstrous book of monsters!

*Alexander Potter  (9)*
*St Bartholomew's CE Primary School, Loughborough*

## DAYLIGHT AND DARK NIGHT

A big blue wall,
Above us all,
The daylight is upon us.

The birds all fly,
Up in the sky,
The daylight is upon us.

The children play,
In the light of the day,
The daylight is upon us.

The people sleep
And dark things peep,
The dark night is upon us.

The sun goes in,
The dark will win,
The dark night is upon us.

All is silent,
All is quiet,
The dark night is upon us.

Day and night,
Dark and light,
The day and night are upon us.

*James Hoyle  (10)*
*St Bartholomew's CE Primary School, Loughborough*

## THE DAY I TOOK A LEMON TO SCHOOL

The day I took a lemon to school,
Everything went wrong.
First, when I hung my coat up,
The peg fell off the wall.
Second was when I sat down,
The chair fell through the floor.
Third, when I got my pen,
The lid flew through the door.
Fourth was when I opened my book,
It disintegrated in my hand.
Fifth was when I was sent to the headmaster,
I accidentally knocked off his toupee.
Sixth was when I was sent home,
The car fell apart.
I put it back together again,
But it would not start.
I took out my lemon
And threw it on the floor.

*William Pearson  (10)*
*St Bartholomew's CE Primary School, Loughborough*

## THE ROLLER COASTER

Up, down and round the track
*Clackity, clickity, clackity clack*
Into the water, put on your mac
Through the tunnel, round the bend
Are we there? Near the end

Up the hill . . . stop then drop
Then you'll go . . . *plop!*
Round and round and round you go
Getting faster

*Whoooo*
Feeling sick yet? Yes I am
Come on, face it, be our man
Do you like this ride? No! I'd rather go on the slide
Then stop!

Let me get off, I feel sick,
Go to the toilet . . . get there quick,
This is the end of this little flick
I was joking, I don't feel sick!

**George Peasant (10)**
**St Bartholomew's CE Primary School, Loughborough**

## SEASONS

*Autumn*
Autumn leaves fall, red, yellow, orange, pink and brown,
Leaves all over, children jumping on piles,
People throwing leaves in the air.

*Summer*
Summer is a good time of year,
The sun shines bright and hot,
Blossoms come back on the trees.

*Winter*
A white sheet on the ground,
People build snowmen,
Snow everywhere.

*Spring*
Birds sing in the trees,
People play in the street,
Flowers peep out of the soil.

**Alexandra Cowley (9)**
**St Bartholomew's CE Primary School, Loughborough**

## SUMMER

Summer
Summer is the best time of year
With birds singing loudly
And rushing deer
The sunny days
Bright green leaves like a swarm of bees
Busy days
When we're on our holidays
A break from school
Where the teachers shout!
When the animals come out from hibernation
And new life is born
Animals appear in big groups
And fruits are ripe like
Plums and strawberries
And tomatoes are as red as cherries
Summer is the best time of year.

*Rhiannon Forrester (10)*
*St Bartholomew's CE Primary School, Loughborough*


## A HORSE VALENTINE

His name is Black Beauty,
He is neighing happily,
Galloping towards a wall, so tall,
He jumps over still neighing with delight,
Big dark eyes, big black wet nose,
He loves to play with all the other horses,
When he jumps, he flies as high as a kite,
But as graceful as a valentine rose.

*Leonie Jenkins (10)*
*St Joseph's Catholic Primary School, Market Harborough*

# CRAZY JUNGLE

Down in the jungle
What will I see?
Leopards singing, 'Wo ho he'.
A monkey swinging from bee to bee
And a snake slithering through a tree.
I could see an orang-utan,
Swinging from a tiger's fang
And a crocodile swimming in a lake,
Eating a big birdie cake.
If I am lucky to find
An anteater with a hairy behind,
Or a giraffe
Having an ice cream bath,
A parrot
Eating a big blue carrot
And lots of hippopotami
Wearing a kipper tie,
What about a bat,
Trying to swallow cowpat,
Or a fish
Eating off a dish.
Down in the jungle,
What will I see?

*Andrew Douglas (8)*
*St Joseph's Catholic Primary School, Market Harborough*

## I AM A DEER

I am a deer, can't you see
I am running around chasing a bee

The hunters are after me, can't you see
I'll hide over here, under a tree

I am now hiding, can't you see
The hunters are no longer after me

The hunters have gone, can't you see
I am as happy as can be

Now I am tired, can't you see
How I hope of being free

I am going to sleep now, can't you see
I never did catch that bumblebee.

*Megan McGowan (8)*
*St Joseph's Catholic Primary School, Market Harborough*


## MY DOG - AJ

My dog, AJ, goes to sleep all day,
When he wakes up, he likes to play.

His best game is 'chase the ball',
He never, ever seems to fall.

He runs and jumps with all his might,
Whilst Mum says, 'Don't let him bite!'

He pushes through bushes and picks up sticks,
After he goes swimming, Dad says, 'He stinks!'

I love AJ best of all,
Because when I'm sad, he brings me his ball!

*Abigail Dockree (8)*
*St Joseph's Catholic Primary School, Market Harborough*

# FOUR LITTLE TIGERS

Four little tigers
Sitting in a tree:
One became a lady's coat -
Now there's only three.

Three little tigers,
B'neath a sky of blue:
One became a rich man's rug -
Now there's only two.

Two little tigers,
Sleeping in the sun:
One a hunter's trophy made -
Now there's only one.

One little tiger,
Waiting to be had:
Oops! He got the hunter first -
Aren't you kind of glad?

*Lauren Sadler  (9)*
*St Joseph's Catholic Primary School, Market Harborough*

## CATS

Cats are whizzy, frizzy things,
They jump about like pogo springs,
I like cats, they're fuzzy wuzzy,
They chase bees, it makes them buzzy.

Cats prowl around,
Like they're the king,
They like to show off
About everything.

Cats jump high,
Cats jump low,
Look out everyone,
Cats on the go.

*Emily Beesley (9)*
*St Joseph's Catholic Primary School, Market Harborough*


## HAPPY AND SAD

When you are happy
You could climb a mountain

When you are sad
You would cry like a fountain

When you are happy
You will smile

When you are sad
You will frown

But best of all
Out of happy and sad
Happy is the best!

*Kate Doncaster (8)*
*St Joseph's Catholic Primary School, Market Harborough*

## MY WORLD

In my world the sky is green
The grass is blue
And no one else is there but you

The hills are small, the rivers high
And you can always touch the sky

You run so slow, you walk so fast
You pick the flowers you're going past

The night is light, the morning dark
And you always hear the singing lark

You're always free, you're never caught
You never have to be taught

It's everything you've ever dreamed
A jump, a shout, but never a scream.

*Samuel Blake (9)*
*St Joseph's Catholic Primary School, Market Harborough*


## HOMEWORK

Homework, homework, homework, I wish it could be banned,
Homework, homework, homework, I'd love it if it turned into sand.
Homework, homework, homework, I'd rather turn into a cat,
Homework, homework, homework, than do some more of that.
Homework, homework, homework, soon you shall see,
Homework, homework, homework, it's as boring as can be,
Homework, homework, homework, soon you shall see,
Homework, homework, homework, is the worst thing known to man!

*Ryan Thompson (11)*
*St Mary's Bitteswell CE Primary School, Lutterworth*

## BUSY BUSINESS

Dad's coming back from his business trip,
So you know what that means . . .
There's gonna be a great hullabaloo
And it will probably be like this:

Mum will be rushing,
Danni will be crying,
I'll be screaming,
The hamster will be hiding.

What a hullabaloo!

Mum will be shouting
Because Danni's squeaking,
I'll be giggling
And the oven buzzing.

What a hullabaloo!

The doorbell will be ringing
And the TV bellowing,
The floorboards creaking,
As Mum goes running
To fetch the baby,
Who is now screeching!

*Stop this hullabaloo!*

**Daisy Seaforth-Craigwell (10)**
**St Mary's Bitteswell CE Primary School, Lutterworth**

## HULLABALOO

Hullabaloo, it's hullabaloo
It's hullabaloo here at school
It's hullabaloo because of my teacher
She lets us loose with some paint and brushes
The reason is we had an extension
The paint was bright pink, purple, blue and green
So we got to work straight away
We found four ladders and climbed up them fast
We had a team leader
That was Ophelia
She told us what, where and when to do it
Everyone had gone mad rushing around
It was complete mayhem
There were people up there and people down here
It was madness, paint falling here and dripping there
But I loved it, painting what I want, where I want
So that's how the day went.

***Georgia Cundick  (10)***
*St Mary's Bitteswell CE Primary School, Lutterworth*

## ICICLES

Hear the icicles dripping from the cave
Hear the icicles going *drip-drop, drip-drop*
Hear the icicles breaking in the wind
Hear the icicles dripping very loudly
Hear the icicles cracking
Hear the icicles freezing very fast
Hear the icicles echo in the cave
Hear the icicles melting at last
Hear the icicles swaying side to side.

***Jarrad Carter  (9)***
*St Mary's Bitteswell CE Primary School, Lutterworth*

## ICICLES

They're claws reaching out to grab you
They're talons dripping blood
They're spears raining down upon you
They're crystal daggers poised to strike

They're embassies of cold, cruel winter
They're frozen flames of frost
They're a portcullis stopping entry
They're ice-covered stalactites but quicker to form

They're swords frozen in mid-stab
They're fangs dripping saliva
They're twisted spires of towers
They're beautiful in their deadly way.

*Alexander Ling (11)*
*St Mary's Bitteswell CE Primary School, Lutterworth*


## MY FRIEND

My friend Alec is a devilish fiend,
My friend Alec is a daring stuntman,
My friend Alec is an enthusiastic bookworm,
My friend Alec is a rugby tackler,
My friend Alec has a pretty girlfriend,
My friend Alec is a fast runner,
My friend Alec is very loyal to me,
My friend Alec is a trustful secret keeper,
My friend Alec is a Beckham boy,
My friend Alec is a cool pop star,
My friend Alec is a computer wiz,
My friend Alec is just like me.

*Jamie Stephenson (10)*
*St Mary's Bitteswell CE Primary School, Lutterworth*

## MY HORSE

I love my horse
And his big brown eyes
A chestnut coloured body
With a white blaze stripe down his nose
I call him my boy
My horse
My joy
Even though his name is Hullabaloo

I love my big horse
And his thick flaxen mane
He never lets me down
Or puts me to shame
With a permanent supply
Of friendly companionship
A presentable posture
He's incredibly fit

I love grooming my horse
The smell of my boy
Then comes to tack
He is just like a toy
Messes about
Round the stable he goes
Now the girth is round his belly
What about his nose?

I love riding my horse
Strong and sturdy he is
A powerful canter
Him and I are the biz
Turn back home
Past the oncoming traffic
Well schooled
Good mannered as well
Oh I love my horse, Hullabaloo

The whole of this poem
Is not quite as it seems
For my horse, Hullabaloo
Is just in my dreams
Could it be possible
That my dream will come true
That I really can ride my own Hullabaloo?

*Emily Wells  (10)*
**St Mary's Bitteswell CE Primary School, Lutterworth**


# I LOVE MY DOG

I love my cute doggy
And her silky brown tail
I love her small paw prints
And her cold, damp nose

I love her big, brown eyes
And her slobbery tongue
I love her black whiskers
And her fluffy brown ears

I love her when she's wet
I love her when she's dry
I love her when she's sleeping
And I love her when she's awake

I love her when she's happy
I love her when she's sad
I love her when she's angry
And even when she's bad.

*Alice Jackson  (11)*
**St Mary's Bitteswell CE Primary School, Lutterworth**

## DANCING HULLABALOO

Tonight is the night
Everything will be alright
I'm getting a bit of stage fright
As the curtains open
And on comes the light
Now the audience are in sight
As I start to dance all over the place
I begin to lose my shoelace
By now I have got a red face
Oh no, what am I going to do?
This is such a hullabaloo
As the lights go down
I begin to frown
I run to meet my mum
I begin to cry
I'm so embarrassed, I'm going to die
Quickly do my hair
Throwing my clothes up in the air
I need to get dressed in a tick
My hair's falling out, I need a hairclip
I think I'm going to be sick
My mum says I'll be brill
If I calm down and chill
If I smile all the while
Then I really will
I got it right, surprise, surprise
My mum's been great, an angel in disguise!

*Olivia Kimberley  (11)*
*St Mary's Bitteswell CE Primary School, Lutterworth*

## WHEN I WAKE UP

When I wake up in the morning
I want to go back snoring
Because I'm tired and I'm sleepy
And I really don't like waking

I put on my slippers and go downstairs
And there I find my teddy bears
It's horrendous, it's a rush
I'm moody and I'm frustrated

I hear the taps running
And the toilets flushing
It's noisy and it's loud
Everybody's rushing around
It's annoying and confusing
I'm getting really angry

I find my shoes
And go back upstairs
I brush my teeth
And do my hair

I must hurry up
Otherwise I'll be late
My mum is now ready
So I must pack my bag

I got in the car
And zoomed down the road
The playground is empty
I'm all alone.

*Helen Swalwell  (9)*
*St Mary's Bitteswell CE Primary School, Lutterworth*

## MY FRIEND

My friend is an angel,
Sent down to Earth,
My friend is a petal,
Off a ravishing, red rose.

She holds her heart out,
For everyone to see,
Her smile is buzzing,
Just like a bee.

She is so thoughtful,
She is so kind,
As she soothes our searching souls,
Every day of the week.

Her hair is in ringlets,
Golden, gorgeous and fine
And her big green eyes
Are shining stars of brightness.

She has blood-red lips,
That are glossy and soft,
This angel is beautiful,
She is my best friend.

*Melanie Lucas  (10)*
*St Mary's Bitteswell CE Primary School, Lutterworth*

# THE TEST

As I watch the time pass by eagerly,
I fiddle with my hair, itch myself nervously,
I chew my pen, cluck like a hen,
My eyes popping purple and green,
My hair static as lightning,
While the teacher demands silence
As she places the paper down,
My face has turned pink with a frown,
I am in a state now, my fingers are going to drop off,
My hard, hot, knobbly hands shaking like a tambourine,
The test I am halfway through, nearly there,
Dreaming of chocolate!
'Five minutes left!' shouts the teacher,
I begin to panic, the person behind me taps their fingers on the table,
*Bang!* goes the door,
The wind whistling down the road,
I am running out of school!
*I am free!*

***Jessica Jenkinson (11)***
***St Mary's Bitteswell CE Primary School, Lutterworth***

## HOMEWORK

I'm sitting on the sofa
Sucking sour sweets
When my mean, miserable mum
Shouts sharply, 'Have you done your history homework?'
I grumble to myself

I rapidly run up the stairs
Staring at the pile of horrible, hideous history homework
I purposely pretend it's not there
Instead I turn on the TV
Quickly but quietly so my
Mean, miserable mum can't hear

She shouts to me
'Turn that terrible TV off
And do your history homework.'
She watches me until I finish
And my horrible, hideous history homework
Wasn't so horrible
So now my lovely history homework
Always gets done first.

*Lucy Fergusson  (9)*
**St Mary's Bitteswell CE Primary School, Lutterworth**

## RUSH HOUR

There's a traffic jam
That goes on for miles,
It goes all the way up the hill,
My mum beeps her horn,
Nothing happens,
Not a single car moves an inch,
Finally we get going
And just when we think it's safe,
Another traffic jam
Comes up at the crossroads,
It looks like we will be here
For quite a long time,
We move again,
We drive towards the train station,
We've got to hurry,
We can't be late,
We've got to pick Gran up,
As we walk inside,
We see it's absolutely packed,
We edge our way through
To platform 9,
Gran greets us,
Then we've got to get back,
We start the impossible task
Of crawling and climbing through the gaps
Of the hundreds of people,
How I hate the *rush hour!*

*Rebecca Peat  (9)*
**St Mary's Bitteswell CE Primary School, Lutterworth**

## WHAT ANNOYS ME!

What annoys me is
My brother watching TV
All old channels
It drives me insane
And Britney Spears music
It's so old
And so not now!
When my mum and dad ask me
To go to bed
'It's only half-eight
I don't want to go yet'
And having homework
Annoys me a lot
I can't work out sums at home
When my brother's friends come round
They wreck my room
I get the blame
They all give me a headache
But what annoys me most is
Action Man, *argh!*

*Jack Tranter  (9)*
**St Mary's Bitteswell CE Primary School, Lutterworth**

## MICHAEL OWEN

Michael Owen came to school
With his magic football
We then went into the hall
And realised he was really tall
He's come to inspect our football team
Because our other inspector isn't too keen
He says we're pretty good
But we don't try as hard as we could
Some say he's weird
But others say he needs a beard
To tell the truth, I quite like him
Even when he gets kicked in the shin
And doubles over in pain
Then screams someone's name
I know he has a red shirt
Apart from when it's covered with dirt
I start to sigh and cry
Because it's time to say goodbye
Although I know he's the world's best football player.

*Abigail Morris (9)*
*St Mary's Bitteswell CE Primary School, Lutterworth*

## THE SNAKE VS THE KANGAROO RAT

The slippery, shiny snake
Is sliding through the dirty, dusty desert,
Looking for his prey.

He saw a kicking kangaroo rat,
Skipping happily in the sand,
While eating a seed.

The snake slithering slowly,
He opens his jaws and . . .
He misses.

The kangaroo rat jumped,
Just in time to save his life
Did the kangaroo rat win?

The snake tried again,
Opened his huge jaw and . . .
*Snap! Snap! Snap!*

The blood was trickling
Down the snake's mouth,
Oh poor little kangaroo rat.

*Beth Hushon  (10)*
**St Mary's Bitteswell CE Primary School, Lutterworth**

## SWIMMING DAY!

I've got to get to school
Even though it's not cool
I look a bit of a fool
Because I fell in the pool
(I get there)
We started to queue up to go to the baths
I'm very glad I miss maths
I pretend to have a good laugh
As we walk past the café
(We get to the swimming baths)
I take off my stuff
As I get in a huff
Because it is tough
Whilst I'm packing my collars and cuffs
(I get in the pool)
We jump in the pool
Splashing around
It's freezing cold but we're having fun
We swim up and down
The whistle blows
(Get out of the pool)
We walk back to class
Cold and dripping wet
The teacher says
'Hurry up, we're late!'

***Emily Haynes  (10)***
***St Mary's Bitteswell CE Primary School, Lutterworth***

## THE VICIOUS VOLCANO

The lumpy lava
Is edging down
The noisy sound
Of the bubbling
Steaming hot lava
Is getting very loud
The terrified villagers
Are funning like
Rabbits away from
The volcanic liquid
It is chasing after them
It's destroying
Everything in its way
Until it reaches
The salty, slimy sea.

*Wesley Boucher  (10)*
*St Mary's Bitteswell CE Primary School, Lutterworth*


## MY BODY

I have toes on my feet
Which I put on my nose!
When I see through my eyes
I will see my hands!
My mouth helps me to eat food . . .
And burp and cough and be sick!
My shoulders go up and down
And sometimes backwards and forwards!
My body wobbles like a jelly
And you feel funny inside your belly!

*Anthony Luckham  (8)*
*St Paul's CE Primary School, Woodhouse Eaves*

## COW AND THE HORSE

The cow and the horse went to France
In a beautiful jazzy plane!
The engine switched off
Everything but the main!
Down, down into the sea they fell
Then suddenly they heard a bell!
It was a killer whale with a bell around its neck
He said, 'My name is Jaws Beck'
But there is no need to be scared!'

*Amelia Selby  (7)*
*St Paul's CE Primary School, Woodhouse Eaves*

## RABBITS

Rabbits are very nice animals
They eat lettuce, grass, carrots and chocolate!
You can even get them orange biscuit treats
They taste like carrots but would poison us!
There are milk buttons that would kills us
But my rabbit likes them as a type of treat!

*Nusaybah Al-Mansouri  (8)*
*St Paul's CE Primary School, Woodhouse Eaves*

## SPY SCHOOL

Spy school is cool
But they can be quite cruel
Because they make you eat lots of gruel!
I like spy school because . . .
I like playing pool after all!

*Adam Spooner  (8)*
*St Paul's CE Primary School, Woodhouse Eaves*

## MY TROPICAL ISLAND

On my tropical island,
You can eat the sand!
On my tropical island,
The birds can talk to you!
On my tropical island,
You can touch the sky!
On my tropical island,
Well, you can do everything!

*Daisy Halligan (8)*
*St Paul's CE Primary School, Woodhouse Eaves*


## SANTA

There is a young man with a beard
He doesn't want anyone to fear
He comes to our house once a year
To see if you are here
Down the chimney he comes
To give presents and lollipops.

*Sophie Lindeman (7)*
*St Paul's CE Primary School, Woodhouse Eaves*


## ONE DAY

One day my mummy took me
Into Loughborough to buy a budgie!
We went to McDonald's – the budgie and me!
I had a cheeseburger and the budgie had a cup of tea!

*Kim Quilter (8)*
*St Paul's CE Primary School, Woodhouse Eaves*

## SCHOOL RULES

Why do people always say they don't want to go to school?
But I am different from all of them,
I think school rules!
My teacher is fun to be taught by
And I'm never shy!
Really, truly throughout these years
School has been so cool!

***Rosalind Barlow (7)***
*St Paul's CE Primary School, Woodhouse Eaves*


## A CROCODILE

A crocodile has a very big mouth,
Teeth and a very bad temper
And you do not want to go near that beast!
If you do, you will wish you did not go there
And before you know it, you will be in that smelly mouth!

***Harriet Lavender (7)***
*St Paul's CE Primary School, Woodhouse Eaves*


## MY FAVOURITE FAIRY

My favourite fairy can fly around
My favourite fairy can touch the ground
My favourite fairy can count to six
My favourite fairy is famous!

***Alice Lathbury (8)***
*St Paul's CE Primary School, Woodhouse Eaves*

## FOOTIE

David Beckham scores a goal!
The crowd goes wild!
No - Ferdinand kicks the ball!
But - David Seaman caught it!
The crowd goes wild!
The crowd goes wild!
The crowd goes wild!

*Maxine Hunter (8)*
*St Paul's CE Primary School, Woodhouse Eaves*


## MY BIKE

My bike is speedy and fast
I can do cool tricks on my bike!
My bike is a mountain bike
I got my bike for Christmas!

*Killian Kirkpatrick (7)*
*St Paul's CE Primary School, Woodhouse Eaves*


## EGYPTIAN MUMMIES

Egyptian mummies are so funny because they are
Wrapped in bandages and left in a tomb to rot!
In the tomb there are some canopic jars
In the jars there are brains and guts
And they stuff the inside with natrom!

*Charlie Keightley (7)*
*St Paul's CE Primary School, Woodhouse Eaves*

## THE SUN

The sun is bright
The sun is hot
The sun is so hot
And so bright as it shines
After the night every day
When I wake up it shines so bright
All day long!

*Clarice Elliott  (7)*
*St Paul's CE Primary School, Woodhouse Eaves*


## SNOW!

Snow is like the moon as it trickles down from the sky.
You can make snow angels, snowmen and much more.
It's soft and fluffy like a pillow and like feathers.
If you feel it – it's cold like ice.
You shiver from the coldness!

*Natasha Hicks  (8)*
*St Paul's CE Primary School, Woodhouse Eaves*


## MY SECRET

Shall I tell you my secret?
Although I have not told anybody,
But I will tell you, if you don't tell anybody!
That's all right, I suppose that's all right.
Now, shall I tell you my secret after all that talking?
So here is my secret, I wish that I could fly!

*Jack Harding  (7)*
*St Paul's CE Primary School, Woodhouse Eaves*

## SWIMMING

S   wimming is slow
W  ater splashes me
I   t's fun to play in
M  ushroom floating is fun
M  uch fun to me
I   wish I could swim every day
N  ice and wet it is
G  reat fun it is

*I love swimming!*

**Natalie Condron  (7)**
**St Paul's CE Primary School, Woodhouse Eaves**


## MY CAT, TOMMY

My cat, Tommy sits on the side!
My cat, Tommy jumps on my leg!
My cat, Tommy looks out my window!
My cat, Tommy plays with a mouse!
My cat, Tommy plays with other cats!

**Oliver Hamilton  (7)**
**St Paul's CE Primary School, Woodhouse Eaves**


## FOOTBALL

I went outside to play football
I played with my dad!
I won and said, 'Yippee!'
So we went inside for a cup of tea!

**Matthew Bettany  (7)**
**St Paul's CE Primary School, Woodhouse Eaves**

## ONE FINE FISH

One fine fish swims in the sea
Got caught, got to *help me!*
Two more fish swim in the sea
One got caught, *help me!*
One fine fish swims in the sea
Got caught, got to *help me!*
That'll be the end of me.

***Adeana Button** (7)*
**St Paul's CE Primary School, Woodhouse Eaves**


## PINK

I like pink baby pigs
I'd like to wear a pink, fluffy wig!
But if I wore it to school it wouldn't be cool
Because the boys don't like pink!
They think it stinks!
But girls like pink and girls rule!

***Hannah Allsopp** (7)*
**St Paul's CE Primary School, Woodhouse Eaves**


## PS2

I've got a PlayStation 2 game
And I play on it all the time.
My brother won a game against me
And I won 1-0 in the end.

***Charlie Breed** (8)*
**St Paul's CE Primary School, Woodhouse Eaves**

# THE SENSES

It was so quiet, I could hear
a spider softly spinning its delicate web.
It was so quiet, I could hear
the dust gently drifting around in the air.
It was so quiet, I could hear
the fur on my pet gently shifting from side to side.
It was so quiet, I could hear
myself silently thinking.
It was so quiet, I could hear
the sun twinkling through the window.
It was so quiet, I could hear
metal rusting.
It was so quiet, I could hear
myself softly dreaming.
It was quiet, I could hear
a snail slowly slithering across the soft leaf.

*Chloe Boulton  (8)*
*Sketchley Hill Primary School*


# THE SENSES

It was so quiet, I could hear
Grass swishing from side to side.

It was so quiet, I could hear
A pebble falling from a mountain.

It was so quiet, I could hear
A butterfly fluttering by.

*Jack Varden  (8)*
*Sketchley Hill Primary School*

## THE SENSES

It was so quiet, I could hear . . .
A spider slowly spinning her web.

It was so quiet, I could hear . . .
A butterfly gliding gracefully in the sky.

It was so quiet, I could hear . .
A rabbit hopping along.

It was so quiet, I could hear . . .
An ant scuttling along the sand.

It was so quiet, I could hear . . .
A dolphin cry softly in the ocean.

***Amy Richardson (8)***
***Sketchley Hill Primary School***


## THE SENSES

It was so quiet, I could hear
A beetle sneaking.

It was so quiet, I could hear
A butterfly flap.

It was so quiet, I could hear
A snake whisper.

It was so quiet, I could hear
A mouse squeak.

***Liam Burchell (8)***
***Sketchley Hill Primary School***

# THE SENSES

It was so quiet, I could hear . . .
A star twinkling.

It was so quiet, I could hear . . .
The sun going down.

It was so quiet, I could hear . . .
My heart beating fast.

It was so quiet, I could hear . . .
A bird flying past.

It was so quiet, I could hear . . .
A horse grazing.

It was so quiet, I could hear . . .
A feather drop.

*Leah Williams (8)*
*Sketchley Hill Primary School*

# THE SENSES

It was so quiet, I could hear . . .
The sun come up and the moon go down.

It was so quiet, I could hear . . .
A cat purring at the end of the street.

*Jasmin Lanford (8)*
*Sketchley Hill Primary School*

## THE SENSES

It was so quiet, I could hear . . .
The grass swishing gently.

It was so quiet, I could hear . . .
People whispering.

It was so quiet, I could hear . . .
A mouse crying loudly.

It was so quiet, I could hear . . .
The leaves on a tree swishing softly.

It was so quiet, I could hear . . .
A snail glide along the ground.

It was so quiet, I could hear . . .
A big book cover crease.

*Jack Heseltine  (8)*
**Sketchley Hill Primary School**


## THE SENSES

It was so quiet, I could hear . . .
Snowflakes falling from the sky.

It was so quiet, I could hear . . .
A bee buzzing in the garden.

It was so quiet, I could hear . . .
A digger moving down the road.

It was so quiet, I could hear . . .
A computer working.

*Sean Tate  (8)*
**Sketchley Hill Primary School**

## THE SENSES

It was so quiet, I could hear . . .
The moon moving in the dark.

It was so quiet, I could hear . . .
The pencil moving on the paper.

It was so quiet, I could hear . . .
A rubber rubbing words out.

*Oliver Taylor  (8)*
**Sketchley Hill Primary School**


## THE SENSES

It was so quiet, I could hear . . .
The soft sand of a child's dream.

It was so quiet, I could hear . . .
The ocean settle softly, far away.

*Tim Bustin  (8)*
**Sketchley Hill Primary School**


## MOLLY AND POLLY

There once was a girl called Molly
Who played with a girl called Polly
They walked down the street
While eating some meat
And found a cute little dolly.

*Lauren Page  (11)*
**Swannington Primary School**

## WINTER

No summer sun, the year is done,
Winter's finally here.
Wrapped up warm, upon the lawn,
The snow starts to appear.

The mice are huddled wearily,
Upon their grassy bed.
So when you are passing by,
On them do not tread.

Ever seen a pin cushion,
Swimming in dead leaves?
It must have taken hedgehog a long time
For this to achieve.

No summer sun, the year is done,
Winter's finally here.
Wrapped up warm, upon the lawn,
The snow starts to appear.

*Thomas MacCalman  (9)*
*Swannington Primary School*


## GHOST

Terrifying ghost
Spirit of a dead person
Ghastly, pasty apparition
Shadow floating in the air
Like smoky clouds
Makes me shiver and run
Like leaves when the wind blows
Terrifying ghost
They can't hurt me.

*Daniel Barnes  (10)*
*Swannington Primary School*

## SNOW

The snow was falling from the sky
Sparkling in my left eye
The fire was burning bright
Giving us warmth and light

Trees were covered with lots of snow
Cats were sitting on branches low
Nobody was still outside
Except a man who needs a ride

Most people were in their beds
Could just make out my five cats' heads
No sledges were speeding down the hill
My brother got a cold and now he's ill.

*Benjamin Salt (9)*
*Swannington Primary School*


## KITTENS

K   ittens so cute and cuddly
I   n my soft, gentle arms
T   izzy and Todd are my favourites
T   heir tiny eyes glaring up at me
E   ager for their food
N   aughty but very playful
S   o beautiful that I love them even more.

*Jasmine Fodczuk (11) & Kristie Edge (10)*
*Swannington Primary School*

## THE SPELL

Gooey, gooey, bubble and chewy
Look, watch, spells are ooey
Colour of a funny snake
In the cauldron we will make
Eye of lizard, head of hog
Wing of bat and tail of dog
Adder's fang and earthworm's slime,
A cat's leg and owlet's chime
For a spell of powerful luck
We will have to add some muck
Gooey, gooey, bubble and chewy
Look, watch, spells are ooey.

***Lorna Hough  (10)***
**Swannington Primary School**


## SNOWDRIFT

Snow, silently drifting down from the wintry sky,
Freezing all lakes and ponds.
Snow, sleepily laying on the soft ground,
Like a million tiny resting sheep.

Snow, making me feel refreshed,
Feeling the frozen breeze.
Snow, like a winter friend,
Leaving as the season passes by.

Snow, silently drifting down from the wintry sky.

***William Underwood & Lewis Causer  (9)***
**Swannington Primary School**

## TWINKLE TWINKLE LITTLE STATION

Twinkle twinkle little station
What about reservation?
The train has arrived
Passengers survived

Twinkle twinkle another train
Why did we turn again?
It was such a calamity
The driver died from TNT!

Twinkle twinkle little station
What about reservation?
The train has arrived
Passengers survived.

*William Salt (9) & Lee Garrett (10)*
*Swannington Primary School*


## MY SPEEDY DIRT BIKE

My speedy dirt bike
Rides on wet mud
Speeding furiously and swiftly
Like lightning
Fast as a Formula 1 car
Makes me feel excited
Like a kangaroo
My seedy dirt bike
Reminds me of winning.

*James Chamberlain (10)*
*Swannington Primary School*

## NIGHTMARE SCHOOL

Bats and spiders everywhere
Quickly glance, no time to stare
Rancid smells creep through the floors
Over chimneys, under doors

Potion testing in the labs
Chemicals burning through the slabs
Bubbling pails, simmering bowls
Constantly creating sausage rolls.

Animal testing very rare
Only come here, if you dare.

*Michael Clark (11)*
*Swannington Primary School*


## FROST

Glittery frost above my head
Cold on my fingertips
Hard, icy, chilly
Like icicles in the air
Like a hard rock laying on the icy ground
Makes me feel like ice inside
Like a shivering tree
Glittery frost above my head
Reminds me of an iceberg.

*Danielle James (9)*
*Swannington Primary School*

## I Don't Know

I have to write a poem
The teacher tells me that I have to try
I feel upset and annoyed
My words get all confused
I don't know why!
I thought it was boring
I didn't want to take part
I think I can't do it
I bet I won't win
I don't know about the ending
How do I begin?
Why should I do it?
What shall I do?
I need to ask for help
She may give me a clue.

*Akash Makvana  (10)*
*Thorpe Acre Junior School*


## Bobbi

My hamster Bobbi is asleep all day
Every night we go to bed
Out she comes to play
When we clean her out, we put her in a ball
And when she's near the steps
We're worried she may fall
When the top falls off her bed
She sleeps in her food
But that's no good because it really puts her in a mood
But I will always love my Bobbi.

*Lauren Axten  (10)*
*Thorpe Acre Junior School*

## FUNNY WORLD

The world is big and round
We have a lot of sound
It's a funny old world though
But how on earth did we get snow?
We can play on a swing
When it gets to spring
And in the warm sun
We can have so much fun
Too quick comes autumn
With the leaves on the ground
Tiny little creatures can now be found
Lots of things happen on this funny old Earth
But one thing's for sure
Everything grows older
From the day of its birth.

*Emmie Bradshaw  (7)*
**Thorpe Acre Junior School**


## THE DRAGON

I am the dragon
Green eyes, long tail
Fiery breath, sharpened claws
Hear my rage, feel my wrath
See my fire that will turn you into ash
Through the bush I await
Smoking breath clogs the air
In my forest trees may stare
I'll be waiting, waiting in my dark lair
Watching you everywhere.

*Daniel Day  (9)*
**Thorpe Acre Junior School**

## THE LAST LEAF

My friends fall from the autumn tree,
I am getting sadder and sadder,
I'm cold up here
I wish it was not autumn
But
It
Is.
I'm sorry for my friends
Falling
Down.
But when a whooshing breeze comes
I will spiral down and fall
From the branches and meet my friends
On the slippy grass and now it's winter
I
Fall!

*Jamie Bailey (9)*
*Thorpe Acre Junior School*


## THE GORGONS

I am the gorgon
I'm a warrior
Moving serpents for my hair
Come and find me if you dare
My eyes can hurt you with one stare
I can kill you, I don't care.

*Chantelle Madondo (10)*
*Thorpe Acre Junior School*

## THE LAST LEAF

I'm all
Lonely,
Sad
And
Cold
Up here,
I'm starting
To lose
My grip and
I'm starting
To flutter and float
Down to the
Green
Ground
Where I'm *happy!*

**Charlotte Orme  (8)**
**Thorpe Acre Junior School**


## THE GORGON

I am a gorgon
Snakes in my head
Hear the snakes slithering out
Hear me roaring, hear me shout
See the clattering of my jaw
Round the bend when you come out
I can sniff you with my snout
Here or there, doors might open anywhere
I will step inside
Your scary nightmare.

**Sabina Chowdhury  (9)**
**Thorpe Acre Junior School**

## RED

Red is like a bunch of lovely roses,
Red is like jelly on a plate,
Red is like a blob of paint,
Red is like anger,
Red is a flame burning down houses,
Red is like blood,
Red is my test book bringing horror on Tuesdays,
Red is danger,
Red is the sunlight just rising,
Red is my school jumper,
Red is a meteor flying through the sky,
Red is my handwriting pen,
Red is my school badge, showing that we care.

*Liam Bradshaw (10)*
*Thorpe Acre Junior School*


## THE MANTICORE

I am a manticore
Half scorpion
With a poisonous body
Hear my call, hear my trumpet
See my sharp teeth, see them shine
In my lair waiting for you
Hear me breathing up the fresh air
Somewhere I am waiting for you
Behind a rock or tree of the jungle.

*Peter Gosling (10)*
*Thorpe Acre Junior School*

## WINTERTIME

W atching my TV inside
I cy windows freezing up
N oble singers coming round
T ime goes fast for hibernating animals
E ating dinners on my own
R acing each other with sleds
T ouching snow every day
I cy roads everywhere
M aking angels in the snow
E veryone is throwing snowballs in my face.

*Rachel Peaty (10)*
*Thorpe Acre Junior School*


## THE GORGON

I am the gorgon
Snakes for my hair
Dark green snakes and blood-red eyes
Hear me slither on the floor
See the statues surrounding me
Behind the statues I live
Blood-red eyes scan the black walls
Somewhere in here a door may whizz open
And I will approach your life
Beware!

*Chandni Khatri (10)*
*Thorpe Acre Junior School*

# THE GORGON

I am the gorgon
I'm a woman
Moving serpents for my hair
Come and find me, if you dare!
My eyes can hurt you with one stare
I can kill you and I don't care!

*Joanne Crane  (10)*
*Thorpe Acre Junior School*


# LIFE

Life is like a flowing stream,
Enjoy every day of your life,
Don't waste it, you will regret it,
Don't be worried about life,
It comes then goes,
Life is like a leaf,
First it's new then it withers and dies.

*Ryan Biddles  (9)*
*Thorpe Acre Junior School*


# SNOW

Snow is like a big fluffy jumper smoothed on the Earth.
Snow is a million white mints scattered on the floor.
Snow is like a big chilly freezer planted in the ground.
Snow is like thousands of white mouldy cornflakes thrown on the floor.
Snow is snow and you can't change that.

*Sarah Mutton  (10)*
*Thorpe Acre Junior School*

## YELLOW

Yellow are the boring books
That I work in all day long
Yellow is the hard chair
That we sit on every day
Yellow is the brilliant sun
That shines and warms my back as I work
Yellow are the fish
Swimming round and round in their tank
Yellow is the sunflower
That brightens up a dull day
Yellow is the bright colour
That puts a smile on my face.

***Thomas Arme  (10)***
***Thorpe Acre Junior School***


## THE GORGON

I am the gorgon
Snakes for my hair
Dark green snakes and blood-red eyes
Hear me slither on the floor
See the statues surrounding me
Behind the statues I live
Blood-red eyes scan the blocked walls
Somewhere in here a door may whizz open
And I will approach your life
Beware!

***Connor Brailsford  (9)***
***Thorpe Acre Junior School***

## NUMBERS, NUMBERS

Numbers are so special, I use them every day,
Numbers are such super fun, they always let me play.

Numbers tell me how tall I am,
Numbers show me how heavy I am.

Numbers help me counting prices,
Numbers irritate me when throwing dices.

Numbers make me divide and add,
Numbers multiplying make me mad.

Numbers, numbers, big and small,
Numbers, numbers, I like them all.

*Luke Pegg  (10)*
*Thorpe Acre Junior School*


## THE GORGON

I am a gorgon
Snakes in my head
Hear the snakes slithering out
Hear me roaring, hear me shout
See the clattering of my jaws
Round the bend when you come out
I can sniff you with my snout
Here or there doors might open
I will step inside your scary nightmares.

*Gemma Jackson  (10)*
*Thorpe Acre Junior School*

## WHAT IS RED?

Red is anger,
Red is blood,
Red is something really not good.
Red is flame,
Red is fame,
Red is something not the same.
Red is the evening and morning sky,
Red, making me think *oh my!*
Red is a robin, chirping as he flies,
Red is a poster on the wall,
Red is a rash, I don't know what to do about it at all
And last of all, I say red is . . . *love!*

*Carrie-Anne Judge (9)*
*Thorpe Acre Junior School*


## THE GORGON

I am the gorgon
I have snake hair
I love to crawl all day long
Hear my hissing echoing
Look at me and you'll turn to stone
Don't shout out cos you're alone
If you face me, you'll be scared
My evil eyes will bring nightmares to life
I scare a lot of people
With my sharp teeth.

*Kharen Amella Birch (10)*
*Thorpe Acre Junior School*

## FLITTER, FLUTTER

Red, yellow, gold
Flittering and fluttering down to Earth
They fall like rain
*Crish, crush* say they
The wind ignores
Giving them a big . . .
*Whoosh*
Up
Up
They fly up
And scatter back down
Have you guessed what they are?

*Alyssa Hunt  (9)*
**Thorpe Acre Junior School**


## THE DRAGON KILLER

I am the dragon
Spiky back too
Vicious teeth and dirty claws
Hear my growling, hear my rage
Touch the poison of my tongue
Over the rocks, hear my scream
Big tail like a scorpion
For here or not, here you will die in pain
And I will enter your world
*Beware!*

*Melissa Woolley  (10)*
**Thorpe Acre Junior School**

## CRAZY KUNG-FU CAT

Riise is the kung-fu cat
When he leaps
It looks like that!
When he rolls, kicks and scratches
He interferes with my football matches!
He gets stuck up trees
He eats like a horse
But he's not big enough for a saddle of course!
He sleeps like a log
Mum says he's lazy
But I know my kung-fu cat is crazy!

*Liam Henson (9)*
*Thorpe Acre Junior School*


## THE GORGON

I am the gorgon,
I have snake hair,
I love to crawl all day,
Hear my hissing, echoing,
Look at me, you'll turn to stone,
Don't shout out 'cause you're alone,
If you face me, you'll be scared,
My evil eye will bring nightmares to life,
I scare a lot of people with my sharp teeth.

*Nakita McDonnagh (10)*
*Thorpe Acre Junior School*

## THE GORGON

I am the Gorgon
Dangerous hair
My eyes turn you into stone
I am a killing machine
I am a woman, don't disturb
In the darkness I shall wait
Now it's time, there is more stone
I am dangerous, keep away or else
I will kill you
Now get out
Away home!

*Matthew Quigley (9)*
*Thorpe Acre Junior School*


## YEAHS AND BOOS!

There's no school today, *yeah!*
But we have to go to the dentist's, *boo!*
We're having a gravy dinner today, *yeah!*
But we have to have cauliflower, *boo!*
We don't have to go shopping today, *yeah!*
But we have to tidy our bedrooms, *boo!*
We can play all day, *yeah!*
But we've got homework to do, *boo!*
We can have sweets today, *yeah!*
But only one, *boo!*

*Georgina Parker (10)*
*Thorpe Acre Junior School*

## SUMMERTIME

S   un is beaming hot
U   nder me is my shadow
M   y breath is running out
M   y body is boiling hot
E   veryone is having fun
R   unning around like lunatics
T   iring their legs already
I   'm very thirsty
M   y mates have had loads to drink
E   veryone has gone home!

*Heidi Lee  (11)*
*Thorpe Acre Junior School*


## FREDERICK

F   ootball Fred
R   olled on his bed
E   ating apple crumble
D   ropped a bit on his lip
E   very time he always tricks
R   hys had a great big tumble
I   picked him up
C   leaned him up
K   evin boiled the kettle.

*Stephanie Pownall  (11)*
*Thorpe Acre Junior School*

## ORANGE

Orange is a ball of fire,
Orange is the bright sun,
Reflected in the shiny river,
Orange is my felt pen that
I write with every day,
Orange is a fish that flashes in the sun,
Orange is a tall pyramid in the Egyptian desert.

*Lauren Esders  (9)*
*Thorpe Acre Junior School*


## STICKY LOLLIES

Sticky lollies everywhere,
On the floor
And in the air,
Eat them cold,
Eat them hot,
Eat them in a month or not,
Sticky lollies in the shops,
Children buying lollipops.

*Zara Bridges  (9)*
*Thorpe Acre Junior School*


## WINTER

Winter comes with turkey baking.
Winter comes with carol singing.
Winter comes with snowflakes drifting.
Winter comes with children snowboarding.
Winter comes with robins perching.

*Monica Matharu  (8)*
*Thorpe Acre Junior School*

## What Is White?

White is a sparkling polar bear drinking water
White is snow falling from the bright blue sky
White is a sink standing in the classroom
White is a whiteboard all clean and new
White is a piece of A4 paper lying on the table
White is a curtain wafting gently in the breeze
White is a T-shirt blowing on the line
White is a handwriting pen, how much will it do today?

*Sophie Brinkworth  (10)*
*Thorpe Acre Junior School*


## Red

Red is some jelly wobbling on a plate,
Red smells like a bright poppy,
Red is a school jumper, fluffy and warm on a winter's day,
Red is a test book bringing dread on Tuesdays,
Red is a handwriting pen, neat or scruffy?
Red is a geography book full of maps and plans.
Red is a . . . ?

*Jodie Taylor  (9)*
*Thorpe Acre Junior School*


## Blue

Blue is the shimmering, glittering sky
Blue is a bird, waiting to fly,
Blue is a winding river, choppy and strong,
Blue is the wind flowing along.

*Micaela Vallance  (10)*
*Thorpe Acre Junior School*

## AT THE BOTTOM OF MY GARDEN

The sun was shining brightly
On this red-hot summer's day
I grabbed my rag doll, Jessica
And we went outside to play

At the bottom of my garden
Sweet singing I could hear
As I got a little closer
It all became quite clear

I crept along the daffodils
Trying not to scare
There sat a little lady
I couldn't help but stare

Her hair was long, like threads of gold,
Her eyes were emerald-green
Two tiny wings upon her back
Her skin so white and clean

'Hello,' I whispered softly
'From where did you appear?'
'I'm a flower fairy!' she replied
'I visit your garden each year

Do you believe in fairies?'
The little lady said
I was so amazed at this beautiful sight
I just smiled and nodded my head

'It's been lovely to meet you and your rag doll
But now I have to fly my dear
Take care of the flowers for me
And I'll be back to see you next year.'

So next time you're in the garden
Listen very carefully
Because you may hear the fairy's song
Who knows what you might see!

*Charlotte Linford (9)*
*Thorpe Acre Junior School*

## THE LAST LEAF

I am on my own
All the other leaves have
Deserted me
And
F
A
L
L
E
N

D
O
W
N

I'm left all alone

One day I will lose my grip
To leave a skeleton tree

I fall just like the others
To make a patterned collage blanket
For the hedgehogs to hide.

*Matthew Beeby (9)*
*Thorpe Acre Junior School*

## SNOW

The white blanket covering the ground
As the children play, wrapped up warm
Rolling up snowballs, making them strong and round
The snow starts to fall once again
The children get excited and run around
As it gets cold the children go in
Sit by the fire
Drinking cocoa
Colouring in the colouring books
And looking at photos.

*Kallum Jamieson  (10)*
*Thorpe Acre Junior School*


## WHAT IS BLUE?

Blue is a puddle
Blue is the sky
Blue is a kite flying up high
Blue is an ocean
Blue is a river
Blue is an ice block making me shiver
Blue is a rainfall
Don't make God cry
Don't let a raindrop fall in my eye.

*Charlotte Simms  (10)*
*Thorpe Acre Junior School*

## LEAF FALL

In summer
The leaves are always
Attached to the trees
But in autumn
When it gets too windy
The leaves can't hold on
So they just f
        a
          l
            l.

***Ben Brooks  (8)***
***Thorpe Acre Junior School***


## THE LONELY LEAF

I'm on my own up here
I'm cold
All my friends are below me
Finally I lose my grip
And the wind blows me
Swiftly d
       o
          w
            n.

***Jessicalin Harvey  (8)***
***Thorpe Acre Junior School***

## WHAT DID YOU DO AT SCHOOL TODAY?

What did you do at school today?
All we did was laugh and play.
What did you do at school today?
All we did was work and say.
What did you do at school today?
All we did was eat lunch and pay.
What did you do at school today?
Boring things like work all day.

*Amy Welstead (10)*
*Thorpe Acre Junior School*


## WHAT IS BLUE?

Blue is the sky floating around and around,
Blue is the carpet staying still on the ground,
Blue is a sparkling waterfall splashing into the sea,
Blue is Heaven singing at me,
Blue is the sea coming up to the shore,
Blue is a car speeding far,
Finally, blue is me.

*Jennifer Smith (10)*
*Thorpe Acre Junior School*


## THE SUN

The sun fled through the sky
It made the stream sparkle
The flowers glow
Puddles dry up
Morning has come.

*Rosie Sutton (10)*
*Thorpe Acre Junior School*

## JUMBLIE

I am Jumblie
Pale green and blue
When I eat my food
I don't half chew

I have small, knobbly knees
Like two frozen peas
See my purple pointy ears
Like horns on deers

I have sharp muddy claws
Like dirty dog's paws
I have spiky yellow teeth
That I use to chew on beef.

*Danielle Preston  (10)*
*Thorpe Acre Junior School*


## THE MANTICORE

I am Manticore, half scorpion
With a poisonous body
Hear my call, hear my trumpet
See my sharp teeth, see them shine
In my hair waiting for you
Hear me breathing up the fresh air
Somewhere I am waiting for you
Behind a rock or tree in the jungle.

*Ryan Mitchell  (10)*
*Thorpe Acre Junior School*